The Relationship-Driven Supply Chain

The Relationship-Driven Supply Chain

Creating a Culture of Collaboration throughout the Chain

STUART EMMETT AND BARRY CROCKER

Published by
Gower Publishing Limited
Gower House
Croft Road
Aldershot
Hampshire
GU11 3HR
England

Gower Publishing Company
Suite 420
101 Cherry Street
Burlington
VT 05401-4405
USA

British Library Cataloguing in Publication Data
Emmett, Stuart
    The relationship-driven supply chain: creating a culture
    of collaboration throughout the chain
    1. Business logistics 2. Corporate culture 3. Interpersonal
    relations
    I. Title II. Crocker, Barry
    658.5

ISBN: 0 566 08684 0

Library of Congress Control Number: 2006923521

Printed and bound in Great Britain by TJ International Ltd, Padstow, Cornwall.

Contents

PART 4   CHANGING AND IMPROVING SUPPLY CHAIN RELATIONSHIPS   135

List of Abbreviations

APS	Automatic Planning and Scheduling
ATO	Assemble To Order
AvD	Average Demand
CAPS	Centre for Advanced Purchasing Studies
CEP	Council on Economic Priorities (US)
CIPS	Chartered Institute of Purchasing and Supply (UK)
CMI	Co-Managed Inventory
CPFR	Collaborative, Planning, Forecasting and Replenishment
CSR	Corporate Social Responsibility
DC	Distribution Centre
DPP	Direct Product Profitability
DV	Demand Variability
ECR	Efficient Consumer Response
EDI	Electronic Data Interchange
ERP	Enterprise Resource Planning
EVA	Economic Added Value
JIT	Just In Time
LCC	Life Cycle Costs
MHE	Materials Handling Equipment
MIT	Massachusetts Institute of Technology
MTO	Make To Order
NDC	National Distribution Centre
OTIF	On-Time In-Full
PCC	Primary Consolidation Centres
QR	Quick Response
RDC	Regional Distribution Centres
RFID	Radio Frequency Identification (of inventory)
ROL	Re-Order Level
S/L	Service Level
SA 8000	Social Accountability 8000
SCM	Supply Chain Management
SKU	Stock Keeping Unit
SLT	Supply Lead Time
SLTV	Supply Lead Time Variability
SMART	Simple, Measurable, Attainable/Achievable, Realistic, Timely (objectives)
TAC	Total Acquisition Cost
TCO	Total Cost of Ownership
TQM	Total Quality Management
VMI	Vendor-Managed Inventory
WLC	Whole Life Costs
WMS	Warehouse Management System

Preface

Our journey to 'today', whilst being an individual one, did not happen without the involvement of other people. On this journey of lifelong learning and meeting people, the original source of an idea or information may have been forgotten. If we have omitted in this book to give anyone credit they are due, we apologise and hope they will contact us so we can correct the omission in a future edition.

To anyone who has ever had contact with us – students, course delegates, clients, colleagues, associates and managers – please be assured you will have contributed to our learning, growing and developing. If you ask us how, then we will tell you! Whilst thanking you all, our hope is that we have given something positive back to you. We are pleased to acknowledge that our learning still continues; indeed writing this book together has certainly contributed to our learning and development.

We have made best endeavours not to include anything in this book that if used, would be injurious or cause financial loss to the user. The user is however strongly recommended before applying or using any of the contents, to check and verify them for themselves and perhaps also with their own company policy/requirements. No liability will be accepted by the authors for any of the contents.

Barry Crocker has a background in UK freight transport and logistics. He entered full time academia in 1988 and is currently the MSc programme leader for Purchasing, Logistics and Supply Chain Management courses at the University of Salford. In addition to this, Barry undertakes training assignments worldwide and has worked with Stuart on many of these. It was during such work that the ideas for the book were formed. Barry has also written and contributed to many distance-learning manuals, has been a CIPS Examiner and is an external examiner for other universities.

Stuart Emmett has a background in freight, warehousing, shipping and international trade and has resided in both the UK and in Nigeria. Since 1998 he has been an independent mentor/coach, trainer and consultant trading under the name of Learn and Change Limited.

Stuart currently enjoys working all over the UK and on four other continents, principally in Africa and the Middle East, but also in the Far East and South America. Additional to undertaking training, he is also involved with one-to-one coaching/mentoring, consulting, writing and assessing, along with examining for professional institutes' qualifications and as an external MSc examiner for Purchasing and Logistics. He can be contacted at www.learnandchange.com.

Foreword

By Alan Waller[*]

Globalisation of supply chains

Companies across all business sectors are extending their geographical reach and influence. Driven by consumer power and economic growth, enabled by freer trade and advances in technology, there are major opportunities for developing new business to meet the changing requirements of a global customer base. In addition, the sourcing of products and raw materials from the best supplier base around the world, increasingly for Western businesses from China as well as Eastern Europe, and the capacity to reach into new markets to achieve business growth, create major new challenges.

As the world changes, supply chains become longer and more complex. This requires a fundamental reappraisal of the way in which businesses manage the total value chain of their products – from raw material to the end customer and final consumer and increasingly including reverse flows.

Supply chain is about raw material sources, it is about packaging sources, it is all the way through primary and secondary manufacturing, finishing, distribution, channels to market. It includes customer service, product returns and recycling. Supply chain management is a professional activity and not a function within an organisation. It needs technology, but technology supports and does not lead.

Supply chain management is strategic and it is also operational. By strategic I mean that a company located in any one country needs to be thinking about global sourcing of raw material and packaging. It needs to think about new markets across the world. It needs to concern itself with the total end-to-end value chain, because the success of the business will ultimately depend on the success of this end-to-end supply chain of which it is only part.

International trade has been around for thousands of years. The difference in skill requirements in today's highly competitive fast-changing world is that we need to have visibility and control of our supply chain in order to compete. Manufacturers need to think upstream about supply and be driven by the end customer. Retailers need to satisfy their customers but need to think supply chain to achieve this. Wal-Mart see their core skill as being 'A procurement agent for the consumer', hence their focus on supply chain management in all they do.

[*]   Professor Alan Waller is President of the Chartered Institute of Logistics and Transport, Vice President of Supply Chain Innovation at Solving International, Director of the European Council on Global Supply Chain in Brussels, Visiting Professor in International Supply Chain Management at Cranfield School of Management and Chairman of the Logistics Directors Forum. Alan is also Chairman of ELUPEG (European Logistics Users, Providers and Enablers Group).

The supply chain is also operational, because the end-to-end supply chain concept has to work, and this is all about getting supply chain thinking and skill-sets into every level of management and supervision, into every business function in every player in the value chain.

The drive for change needs to come from the top, and the leadership of change to convert supply chain thinking into operational best practice must be taken up as a boardroom responsibility.

Global supply chains need to provide competitive costs in getting the products to market. It makes little sense to choose a manufacturing location that has cost-effective labour, low investment costs and high subsidies if the cost, time and risk involved in delivering the product to the marketplace more than eliminates those advantages. Total manufacturing and distribution costs and reliability of supply must match those of competitors.

Outsourcing is central to sustaining focus on core competence and competitiveness, and can reduce complexity and mitigate uncertainty. However, attitudes to outsourcing must change and the focus should now be on creating partnerships. With estimates that within the next year or so more than half of supply change management functionality will be provided by partners outside the enterprise, we must all get better at managing this key business process. Genuine collaboration is the route to the future.

Information technology and people skills

Before the development of today's information technology capability, supply chains had to be constructed so that the physical flow of goods followed and was consistent with the flow of information. Now we have the IT capabilities to develop the physical supply chain without such constraints. This provides opportunities in the way the physical assets of the supply chain are deployed. Supplier facilities, manufacturing plants, outsourced operations and distribution facilities can all be restructured into a radical new supply chain capability, with technology supplying real-time, visible access to demand and supply information.

IT systems, and particularly the Internet, now offer capabilities undreamed of a decade ago. Enterprise resource planning systems from providers such as SAP, Oracle and PeopleSoft are augmented with supply chain planning and execution systems from companies like Manugistics and i2. However, we need to be realistic about the maturity of the systems that have emerged and our ability to exploit them.

Through to the end of the last millennium, the constraint to progress in implementing world-class supply chain management solutions had been the lack of appropriate technology. As we have moved into this new millennium, it has become increasingly clear that the availability of technology is no longer the key constraint.

The focus now must be to move to developing the organisational capability to exploit this technology and to working with other businesses to make the internal and external cross-enterprise supply chain effective. All this in parallel with ensuring appropriate people skills, from chief executive to transport manager, that equip individuals with not only the appropriate depth of expertise to get their own job done, but also the breadth of supply chain understanding to ensure joined-up supply chain thinking and actions, through from strategic direction to operational performance.

We need T-shaped managers at all levels in all value chain businesses.

Managers need to be good at their job, but they need to be broad enough to think and act supply chain, both internal to their own organisation and also externally between their organisation and the other players that make up the value chain and on whom they depend for success. Companies and managers should be thinking 'If they fail, I fail'.

Logistics and supply chain are new concepts, emerging only in the 80s and 90s to have any true meaning. Supply has a connotation of being a push system, and for many the 'demand chain' is more meaningful. These concepts are being combined as 'the demand-driven supply chain'. But chains are being replaced by networks or webs, and so we are struggling with trying to find new expressions to demonstrate how our thinking and practice in the application of the 'logistics' concept is moving forward. So why do we need to bring in a concept like 'the relationship-driven supply chain'?

As Director of the European Council for Global Supply Chain for The Conference Board in Brussels, I have been working with council members to identify the factors driving the 'Supply Chain of the Future'. We have highlighted the 12 major drivers of change and 'people, organisation and skills' has emerged as the number one priority driver – and response – for the future shaping and success of the supply chain.

In the surveys that I have carried out across Europe over the past 15 years, the obstacles to progress used to be about technology – 'The availability of appropriate IT systems and communication technology'. This has now all changed. The quote that came through from my latest survey in 1993 was: 'We have all the technology we need – what we need now is to ensure we can use that technology effectively.' Now, the biggest barrier is the availability and deployment of appropriate people and organisational skills. The need for T-shaped people working in T-shaped organisations.

The T-shaped person has an upright I skill-base or expertise in his or her chosen speciality. The cross-bar on the T is about understanding the supply chain and having the skills to get functions within the organisation, and businesses across the end-to-end supply chain, to work together. We're very good at developing I-shaped experts. What's now important is to turn all our managers – and directors – into T-shaped people and develop the supply chain skills across the value chain.

The T-shaped organisation has an upright 'I' representing the focus on the core competence of the organisation. The cross-bar on the 'T' is about understanding the extended value chain and being able to understand and influence supply chain partners to work to the benefit of the total value chain across all enterprises. It is about making collaboration work.

'Act production, act brand management, act procurement, act selling – but think supply chain.'

We have been taught how to compete, but no-one has taught us how to work together.

I set up ELUPEG in response to European businesses who urgently needed an independent forum where they could work on collaborative projects to improve the service and cost performance of European logistics. In the extensive survey that I carried out before doing this I asked the question, 'Who should take the initiative in pushing forward these types of activities?' The reply was clear: users must take a lead, but logistics providers and enablers – such as consultants – are essential to make it happen. In short, the only way forward was a collaborative approach. Hence the focus in ELUPEG on inclusivity and the development of relationships between supply chain players so that businesses can work together to take initiatives from concept to full implementation.

The concept of 'the relationship-driven supply chain' is an important move forward to bring relationship management between organisations to the fore.

Introduction

We have four parts to this book:

- Part 1: The supply chain reviewed
- Part 2: People relationships at work
- Part 3: Supply chain relationships in business
- Part 4: Changing and improving supply chain relationships.

A word of advice is needed on this content ordering. The very nature of the supply chain requires integrating and connecting at different levels. As a parallel, readers will need to iteratively integrate and connect their study of this book to enable a more complete and full understanding of it.

'Extremes' and 'ideal-typical' views

These are used in the book to stimulate debate and discussion. They present polarised black/white views. They are not intended to be a 'good' or 'bad' comparison. The reality and the practice will be found in the 'grey' between the 'black/white' extremes. Also, some aspects can be mixed between the two extremes.

Asking questions

Peter Drucker, the well-known and arguably best management guru, has observed that the problem with Western managers is the emphasis of finding the right answer rather than asking the right question. Asking right questions generates right answers. Therefore we present many questions in this book, some being in the form of checklists. They are designed for answers of practical application to your circumstances and organisation.

Relationships and collaboration

In this book, we would support and wish to further the view of Alan Waller (President of the Chartered Institute of Transport and Logistics, Chairman of the European Logistics Users, Providers and Enablers Group, and Visiting Professor at Cranfield Centre for Logistics and Supply Chain Management) who in summary has stated:

The supply chain lies no longer with an individual company; we have global networks cutting across countries and organisations. The only way to achieve this is to get players working to a common agenda – the collaboration agenda. We have been taught to compete: nobody has taught us to work together. The need and awareness is there but still nobody has taught how to do it.

Our hope is that this book takes Alan Waller's views further and gives some very specific and definite ways forward.

The supply chain: A new phrase?

It does seem that some are in danger of using the supply chain as a new phrase that can be variously substituted for procurement/buying or for transport/ logistics. However, these management areas alone are not the only specialised provinces covered by the supply chain.

We need to always remember the wider and holistic views that supply chain management is meant to afford and contribute. Our view in this book is very clear: that supply chain management is a philosophy and a way of looking at how to better manage across functions.

If we try to make supply chain management a functional department, then we will run the risk of subordinating the benefits of the approach and getting locked into power plays and the playing of serious schoolyard politics; such matters being commonly found in and between existing organisational functional silos/departments. Supply chain management by definition is all about integrating, coordinating and control, across internal and external functions.

The Supply Chain Reviewed

> *The focus of supply chain management is on cooperation and trust and the recognition that properly managed, the whole can be greater than the sum of its parts.*
>
> Martin Christopher: *Logistics and Supply Chain Management* (1998)

In Part 1 we define what the supply chain is. This leads us onto discussing supply/demand/value chains and how there are many different types of supply chains. Whilst different companies and industries will have differing expectations, competitive advantage can be a key output from any supply chain.

An important point that we establish early is that for effective management of supply chains, there is a need to work together, both internally in an organisation and also externally with suppliers/customers. Additionally, inventory is a common component in every product supply chain and requires joint management approaches.

We next look at the history and development of supply chain management (SCM) and how the philosophy has grown in parallel with changes in technology and business approaches. Benefits of effective SCM are well documented as costs are reduced and service improves; the best of both worlds can be achieved as inventory levels are reduced, on-time in-full (OTIF) deliveries are made and profit increases. This comes from recognising and acting on what we see as the five key areas of SCM for any organisation: lead time, customer service, adding value, trade-offs and information. We next examine varied approaches to SCM and look at the value chain, the theory of constraints and lean/agile approaches.

We have by now established the 'case' and the need for SCM. We continue by exploring how it will change traditional ways, for example from independence to dependence, from interfacing to integrating and from supply to demand chains.

We then compare the transactional approach with the collaborative approach using criteria of price/risk, negotiations, interpersonal relationships, trust and controls. We also briefly examine the roles of power and the hard/soft management skills, both of which are explored more fully later in the book.

Next we compare and contrast what we call Type I and Type II supply chains; the former being more about production-led supply push and the latter being more about market-led demand pull. Criteria used in this comparison are main drivers, products, inventory, buying, making, moving, customers, information, handling of orders, lead times, costs, price and organisation methods.

The supply chain operational areas of procurement, production, distribution and marketing are then looked at to see how they need to relate to each other for effective SCM and overcoming problems in integrating such operations are briefly explored. Supply chain strategy, planning, design, key performance indicators and the monitoring of strategy are discussed. Finally in this part we review the alternative supply chain strategies.

Part 1 therefore presents a view of what fundamentally the supply chain is, what it can do and how it needs to be integrated. The rest of the book takes this forward, by examining the relationship-driven supply chain and how to create a culture of collaboration.

The supply chain

The 'supply chain' is the process that integrates, coordinates and controls the movement of goods, materials and information from a supplier through a series of intermediate customers to the final consumer.

The essential point with a supply chain is that it links all the activities between suppliers and customers to the consumer in a timely manner. SCM therefore involves the management of buying/sourcing, making, moving and selling activities.

Following from the initial customer/consumer demand, the supply chain is then what 'takes care of business'. Indeed, nothing happens with the supply until there is an order/demand; it is the order that drives the whole process. Some people logically argue that the term supply chain could be called the demand chain.

So the supply chain bridges the gap between the fundamental core business aspects of supply and demand, as shown in Figure 1.1.

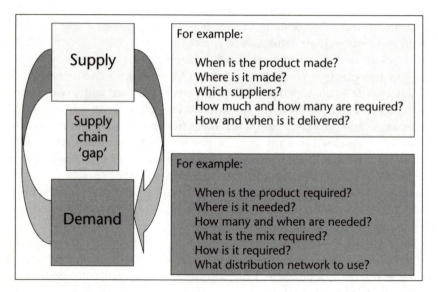

Figure 1.1   The supply chain bridges the gap

The philosophy underpinning SCM is to view all these independent processes as being related holistically and interdependently, so that they:

        integrate, coordinate and control

        the movement of materials, inventory and information

        from suppliers through a company to meet all the customer(s) and the ultimate consumer requirements

        in a timely manner.

A diagrammatic view follows in Figure 1.2 where it will be seen that the flows of products and the flows of information are represented by ideas, order creation, and cash/orders.

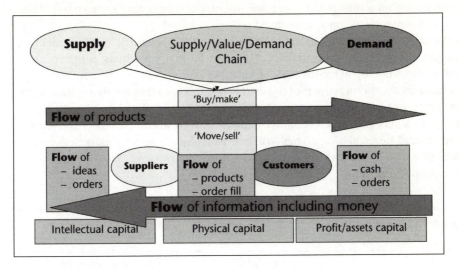

Figure 1.2   Flow of products and information

In the diagram, the views of demand/supply/value chains are shown:

- The demand chain represents the creation of demand; for example, marketing and selling with product development.
- The supply chain represents fulfilment; for example, procurement and buying, production and making with distribution and moving.
- The value chain represents performance; for example, financial measures and capital.

The activities of buying, making, moving and selling take place in the operational functions of purchasing, production, distribution and marketing, respectively. If each of these functions were to work independently, then inventory stock levels will increase not only internally, but also across the supply chains that feed in and out from a company.

It is also important to realise that each company has not one supply chain, but many, as it deals with different suppliers and has different customers. For each individual finished product or line item, whilst some of the buying, making, moving and selling processes will be identical or very similar, the total supply chain for each product will be different and will involve often a complex network. This network also goes, for example, far beyond the first supplier and includes the supplier's supplier, then that supplier's supplier and so on.

Many companies with their SCM do not actually operate the supply chain like this and often stop with their first-level supplier. They seem to forget that the supply chain is effectively a larger network of supplier/customer players and that fuller integration, beyond both the internal activities and the first-level suppliers, can bring increased benefits.

This can be a reflection of how different types of business and industry sectors view the supply chain. For example:

- Retailers are driven by customer demand creation requiring the stocking, availability and fulfilment of a wide variety of finished and consumable products. They will stock products for the minimum time possible and will use suppliers who have varied production options of 'make to stock', 'supply from stock' and 'pack to order'.
- Oil companies are driven by oil production; so the supporting of oil production by the supply side is of utmost importance. Therefore for many products, suppliers manufacture products using the make-to-stock production option. This is then followed with stock holding by the oil companies of finished goods stock, so that goods are always going to be available 'just in case' they are needed.
- Car assemblers are more consumer demand driven, meaning closer integration of the supply and demand sides. They will use assemble to order production options using suppliers who have synchronised and scheduled make/assemble to order options and who can supply 'just in time' (JIT).

Businesses may be classified as follows to show the influences of their operating environment; the key driver is highlighted:

	High complexity	Low complexity
High uncertainty	Capital-intensive industries: Aerospace Shipbuilding Construction **Fitness for purpose** (of product)	Fast-moving consumer goods: Cosmetics Textiles Food and drink **Time to market**
Low uncertainty	Consumer goods: Automotive White goods Electrical goods **Value for money**	Staple primary industries: Paper Glass Simple components **Price** (from production productivity)

Supply chains differ, therefore; multiple SCM is perhaps a better description, although this is a cumbersome term.

At a simple level, consider the supply chain (part only) for Lee Cooper jeans that has customers located worldwide (accessed via agents, wholesalers and retailers), from a factory in Tunisia, that gets supplies of:

- denim cloth from Italy, who use dye from West Germany and cotton from Benin, West Africa and Pakistan;
- zips from West Germany, who use wire for the teeth from Japan and polyester tape from France;
- thread from Northern Ireland, who use dye from Spain and fibre from Japan;
- rivets and buttons from the USA, who use zinc from Australia and copper from Namibia;
- pumice (used in stonewashing) from Turkey.

With SCM therefore, there are many different supply chains to manage. These supply chain networks will contain companies from all the following main sectors:

- *primary sector* – raw materials from farming/fishing (food, beverages and forestry), quarrying/mining (minerals, coals, metals) or drilling (oil, gas, water);
- *secondary sector* – conversion of raw materials into products: milling, smelting, extracting, refining into oils/chemicals/products and then machining, fabricating, moulding, assembly, mixing, processing, constructing into components, sub-assemblies, building construction/structures and furniture/electronic/food/paper/metal/chemicals and plastic products;
- *service or tertiary sector* – business, personal and entertainment services which involve the channels of distribution from suppliers to customers via direct, wholesale or retail channels. Services include packaging, physical distribution, hotels, catering, banking, insurance, finance, education, public sector, post, telecoms, retail, repairs, and so on.

Companies will therefore have many supply chains both internally and externally that interact through a series of simple to complex networks.

These networks can be domestic, international or global in reach. As Ronald Reagan once famously said, using an earlier quotation from *The Gutenberg Galaxy* (1962) by Herbert Marshall McLuhan, 'We now live in a global village.'

FLOWS OF MATERIALS AND INFORMATION AND MONEY

In organising the material flows from any national, international or global locations, then the following will be required:

- forecasting of the demand requirements;
- sourcing and buying from vendors/suppliers. At some stage, in the supply cycle, there will be a manufacturer/producer involved. These may possibly be well down the supply chain when the supplier is an agent, a trader or a wholesaler or some other kind of middle person;
- transport;
- receiving, handling, warehousing and, possibly, storing.

The material flows are triggered by information, as information is needed for decision making. Information is also used to:

- implement other activities
- plan
- organise
- direct and coordinate
- control.

Information flows therefore link internal company activities and also link external suppliers and customers. Effective information and communication technology (ICT) will process orders, track and trace progress and provide timely and real-time visibility. The supply cycle information loop covers:

- forecasts
- buying
- purchase order and transactions
- stock information.

The demand or customer cycle information loop covers:

- stock information
- replenishment and picking/order assembly
- transport and delivery
- invoicing
- payment.

The integration of the supply and demand information loops gives an integrated system.

It will be seen also that money flows are also involved as information integrates materials and money flows. The design of the supply chain will determine the following monetary aspects:

- asset investment (for example, this is minimised by outsourcing)
- inventory holding and carrying costs (for example, from decisions on stock holding policy)
- debtor balances (for example, the customer order cycle times)
- creditor balances (for example, from holding lower stock levels)
- exchange rate variations from non domestic trade (for example by balancing the material flows).

It is in the planning, organising and controlling of these total material flows that SCM provides competitive advantage. This is why Martin Christopher, the UK's eminent professor specialising in the supply chain, notes that the future is one of competing interdependent supply chains and not from individual companies operating independently.

Individual companies therefore need to work together to manage the flows. These flows are determined by demand; therefore demand pulls the product, which in turn needs a flexible response from upstream, so as to satisfy the downstream information flows demand. Supplier bases may therefore have to be rationalised, as not all will be able to provide any new requirements for flexible, on time, in full deliveries; the requirement for demand-driven supply chains.

START AT HOME

The starting point with SCM however, must be to first examine the internal supply chain. Many companies however start SCM (with much time and effort) by working only with the closest suppliers and customers. They should however first ensure that all their internal operations and activities are integrated, coordinated and controlled. Companies may usefully ask their suppliers and customers whether the internal supply chain is working well; they may be surprised by the answer.

MANAGE THE INVENTORY

In the supply chain then, the flows of goods and information will need coordinating to minimise inventory levels. High levels of inventory can be viewed as a major symptom of an ailing supply chain that needs to be treated.

Consider for example, the minimal stock holding of parts and components held by car assembly companies. They have minimised stock levels in the chain by working with the first tier suppliers and also the first tier supplier suppliers. As noted above, in SCM there are many different supply chains to manage and these supply chains will usually contain companies in many different sectors; all of these companies in the network can hold excess inventory.

As has been said in SCM, holding stock can be an admission of defeat as this reflects the view that stock holding is anti-flow and can be analogous to water flowing. Water does not always flow evenly and at the same pace everywhere along a stream. Water sometimes gets trapped in deep pools, is blocked by rocks and other obstacles hidden below the surface. These rock and obstacles impede the smooth swift flows of the stream. Here the stream represents the flow of goods and information in the supply chain and the pools of water are the inventory holdings. The rocks/obstacles represent the waste in the process from poor quality, returned goods, re-ordering and so on. If a stream is to flow fast and clear, then the rocks and obstacles have to be removed. To do this, the water (and inventory) level has to be lowered so that the rocks are exposed.

Inventory can therefore be hiding more fundamental problems than is immediately apparent. As such inventory can be seen as the 'root of all evil' in the supply chain and be an admission of defeat for SCM. This is not to say that all inventory is incorrect and wrong, some will be needed and may be essential to facilitate processes. It is the level and amount being held that is being challenged.

Inventory is therefore the common component throughout the total supply chain, the format being raw material, sub-assemblies/work in progress or finished goods (which are often held at multiple places in the supply chain). Where it is held is of common interest to all supply chain players, as the cost of holding inventory has to be paid for (built into the selling price), usually by the next downstream player. Inventory holding must therefore be jointly investigated and examined.

Let us now look at how we can break down some of the barriers in supply chains to allow more collaboration in integrated supply chains.

INTEGRATION OF THE SUPPLY CHAIN – BREAKING DOWN BARRIERS

When you start to look at traditional supply chains that have not been re-engineered for competition, there are barriers between the departments in a company, between the company and its customers, its customers and their customers, and there are barriers between a company and its suppliers.

The role of management in SCM is to remove the barriers between the company and its suppliers and even perhaps its suppliers' suppliers.

There are formal structures set up to get things over and through the barriers, but the barriers generally stay in place. Where companies do not bother to develop formal structures, individuals may chip holes in the barriers and create informal structures so that they can do their jobs more easily.

On the other hand, the barriers may be put up even higher in order to hide actual costs, to protect proprietary knowledge, to keep resources on one side of the fence or because companies develop confrontational styles of interaction and want to hide from each other, except for once a year when they sit and negotiate a new contract. But whether the barrier stays the same, gets a bit higher or has a few holes created in it, nobody questions that barrier. This is because, for example, a jam manufacturer and the jar manufacturers are isolated units, and it is assumed that they have to operate as such.

In a world-class supply chain, these barriers cannot remain. It cannot be that the flow of product, information and finances between the links in the chain are allowed to be compromised by the perception of company boundaries. Despite the fact that supply chains are made up of different companies and that there may be both legal restrictions and operational difficulties, these must all be overcome so that the supply chain is treated as a whole and is optimised as a whole.

The contrast to this is to optimise the short-term profitability of individual links, to the detriment of the overall supply chain, which results in a sub-optimal solution for everyone in the supply chain. Competition is more often than not about having the flexibility to satisfy a customer's unique demands, which requires the tight coordination of the different links, modules, departments or companies throughout a supply chain – whatever their ownership.

Competitiveness therefore depends on the supply chain, not on any one link.

COSTS

The cost discussion can and has gone many ways. In recent recessions, companies attempted to drive out cost by restructuring their own internal practices. This often involved a great deal of automation, in which for example a procurement department played a role. There are many procurement departments, which have contributed to cost reduction processes by automating their ordering processes with suppliers. There are probably many more that have been involved in cost reduction exercises in terms of negotiating down the standard costs for bought-in services, components and raw materials.

In a recession, however, it means we tend to be looking for cost reductions that are associated with the development of lean supply chains. This means that rather than automating internal processes, companies are looking for the efficiencies that come from making the whole work better as a whole, or in other words, optimisation of the whole rather than its parts.

There is a huge element of cost to be removed through:

- reducing waste in and between all links (especially wasted time);
- reducing inventories;
- reducing write-offs;
- decreasing administration;
- decreasing handling;
- decreasing transportation costs.

CHANGED ROLES

Achievement of these lean supply chains leads to world-class competitiveness and the role of individual organisational departments in achieving this is very different than the roles outlined above. Here, the role of procurement, for example, is to integrate the supplier into the supply chain and then work to ensure that the supplier is involved in optimisation of the whole. This can mean either changing the activities at the suppliers, changing the links between suppliers and other parts of the chain, or by using supplier resources to change activities elsewhere in the chain. The role of procurement becomes fundamentally different in that it does not look in on the function, but on the impact on the supply chain.

If the supply chain is tightened up as discussed above, with time and inventories taken out and information flows greatly improved, there is a great deal of scope for increasing the responsiveness of the chain to the customer's requirements; and increased responsiveness should mean increased customer satisfaction.

As an absolute minimum, each member of the supply chain needs to get a sufficient enough return to keep going (given that there are continuous incentives for performance improvement). It is likely that such a return has to stimulate continued interest in and innovation for the supply chain; part of the supply chain philosophy has to be win-win.

It is the role of SCM to break down the barriers between a company and its suppliers. This process involves four elements:

- changing the corporate perception of the supplier as a separate entity;
- increasing the visibility of information throughout the supply chain;
- redesigning the supply chain so that activities are carried out most effectively;
- initial design of the supply chain for proper management.

The first point is fundamental: the organisation has to change the way it thinks about its relationship with suppliers. Many companies have gone a long way towards this with the implementation of collaborative ideas. But collaboration cannot be like the Trojan horse that gets in through the barrier (using declarations of good tidings), takes what is there and then gets out.

It cannot be restricted to any single company function, like procurement. If the whole company does not buy into the importance of developing suppliers as collaborative partnerships, it just will not happen. It will not happen because the departments in the company will not free up the resources required to work with the suppliers in collaborative partnerships. It might be that it does not top their priority list, or they absolutely block developments on the basis of needing to protect the company. It is not easy to fight years of precedent. The role required here is one that makes the company understand that the suppliers, as a link in the supply chain, are at least as important as their own company; the role is to develop true collaboration between the companies.

If members of a supply chain are going to have a fighting chance of contributing to an overall effective system, they have to be allowed access to information on forward demand through the system. If that information is not available, it has to be made so by getting those parties in touch with the market more involved and communicative. The more factual that time information is throughout the supply chain the more responsive it can be – given good information.

A major recent buzzword has been the re-engineering of processes for greater efficiency and responsiveness. This basically means that activity chains have to be re-evaluated, so that activities take place in the most effective way for the supply chain. Quite often this means that we look for opportunities to carry out activities early on in the supply chain so as to avoid repetition later. For example, the jar manufacturer may clean the jars and then seal them with the final lid, as the manufacturer used to do. The jam manufacturer would then operate a system of open – fill – seal, rather than wash – assemble – fill – seal. The system could be redesigned so that the jar manufacturer puts their jars in a 36-jar container that is properly coded to be read throughout the supply chain (transport, through the filling line, transport and warehousing again, and then transport to the retailer). The jars might not have to leave the same container until they reach the supermarket and are sold on to the consumer.

Perhaps one of the most telling examples of getting activities to occur most effectively in the supply chain is the generic issue of quality control. For example, the quality of the jars should be checked during the production process at the jar manufacturer, not in the jam manufacturer's facilities. Problems should be solved in the supplier's process, not on the jam manufacturer's line.

All this requires resources to be available to the supplier, from the customer company or elsewhere if necessary. It will then, for example, become the responsibility of SCM to ensure that the suppliers receive the resources they require. It is also responsible to determine the financial implications of any changes; this may require entirely different skills such as value analysis.

Conversely, it could be argued that it is the role of SCM to make sure that the resources of the supplier, whether they are technical, commercial or whatever, are allowed to benefit the customer company or further up the supply chain. Too often the supplier's expertise is not fully utilised due to internal resistance by some department that wants to protect their own power base.

JOINT DESIGN

Products and processes have to be designed so that:

- they can be manufactured;
- they can be distributed;
- feedback from the customer regarding the output can be moved back throughout the supply chain in a timely way;
- the next customer receives a more tailored response.

Again this requires information throughout the chain, but it also involves barriers being removed: the supply chain has to allow the development resource to go where it is most needed. For example, it is no good improving the flavour of the jam if you cannot get the jar open.

This means that all parties should be involved in the design of the supply chain from the beginning, such that the best resources are applied to the question, as well as making sure that the solution works for all the involved parties. More bluntly, wrong solutions should not be imposed on parties that could have contributed to good solutions. In procurement for example, this means working within their own organisation and allowing suppliers into the design process at the very beginning. It may be that procurement has to look for or cultivate suppliers that have the capability to take over and maintain responsibility for a key component of the ultimate design – and then to convince their own company that others may be much more suitable to provide that service than their own R&D people. The role of procurement here therefore includes to coordinate and to champion the input of the supplier into the process.

Companies that have accomplished the following four things have managed to remove the barriers between themselves and their suppliers:

- shared perceptions of suppliers as a fundamental part of the supply chain;
- visibility throughout the chain;
- efficient and responsive systems;
- product development for SCM.

SUMMARY

The final customers do not differentiate between different stages of the supply chain. They do not differentiate between quality problems that originate with the manufacturer of the product or its suppliers. There is no-one saying 'Well, it was not their fault, they did not produce the jam jar, it was their lousy supplier.' Nor is any customer going to excuse late delivery because a supplier further up the supply chain did not supply within or outside of lead time.

Nor does anyone excuse a lack of innovation because a company did not happen to make use of a particular supplier's design capabilities. As unreasonable as it may seem, the final customer is only interested in the goods or services presented to them at the end of the supply chain.

The supplier is an integral part of the offering to the final customer, and the role of SCM is to take down the barriers between the company and its suppliers so that the supplier contributes to efficient and effective flexible systems that maximise customer satisfaction at a mutual benefit in terms of cost, overall profit and added value.

Supply chain history

Some barriers have historically been removed, and in the UK the history of the supply chain can be viewed as passing through three phases. However, with any such stereotyping there is much overlap. However, such an 'ideal-typical' view enables key areas to be viewed more clearly.

Attribute	Functional supply chains To the 1980s	Responsive supply chains The 1990s	Adaptive supply chains The 2000s
Integration focus	Over the wall Reactive/quick fixes Monopoly suppliers	Transactional Responsive Competition in suppliers	Collaboration Decision/proactive Joined-up networks of enterprises
Customer focus	Customer can wait 'You will get it when we can send it'	Customers wants it soon 'You will have it when you want it'	Customer wants it now 'You will get it'
Organisation focus	Departmental and ring fencing	Intra-enterprise 'Internal' involvement	Extended enterprise involvement
Product positioning	Make to stock Decentralised stock holding Store then deliver	Assemble to order Centralised stock holding Collect and cross dock (transit handling with only 'hours' of storage)	Make to order Minimal stock holding Whatever is needed
Management approach	Hierarchical	Command and control	Collaborative
Technology focus	Point solution	ERP	Web connected

Attribute	Functional supply chains To the 1980s	Responsive supply chains The 1990s	Adaptive supply chains The 2000s
Time focus for the business	Weeks to months	Days to weeks	Real time
Performance focus	Cost	Cost and service	Revenue and profit
Collaboration	Low	Medium	High levels
Response times	Static	Medium	Dynamic

Supply chain growth

Supply chains have grown like the UK road system. Roads developed over time from basic tracks between local supply and demand centres and they tended to be built in line with the environment taking an indirect route; for example, around hills and down valleys. This contrasts with more recent motorway networks that now give more direct movements with a complex and holistically designed network that also separates out fast and slow movers.

The developments in roads and in SCM have therefore been similar:

- simple to complex
- indirect to direct
- mixed to separated flows
- slow to fast movement.

As supply chains have grown and developed, there have been many words used to describe SCM, and the following can be observed. Again, the following stages overlap and they are not mutually exclusive.

Main concentration and aim	Names used and time period	Flow type and the main parts involved
Sheds/trucks	Warehousing and transport is 'separated' 1950s	Physical flows 'Move'
Physical networks and inventory reduction	Physical distribution management (PDM) 1960s	Physical flows 'Move'
Centralised inventory	Material management + PDM 1970s	Physical flows 'Buy-make-move'
Eliminate inventory	Logistics management 1980s	Physical + information 'Buy-make-move-sell'
Continuous replenishment	SCM 1990s	Physical + Information 'Buy-make-move-sell'
Zero lead time and total visibility	Demand pipeline management 2000s	Physical + Information 'Buy-make-move-sell'

Whether the expression 'demand pipeline management' will become common remains to be seen. However, it does reflect that the supply is initiated by demand and that, without demand, there is no supply chain. Additionally, the pipeline analogy can be useful as one of the main aims for SCM is the smooth flows of goods and information that are instantly available 'on tap' from a pipe. This analogy however should not be taken to suggest that the supply chain represents a linear and seamless fixed pipe with a stable, controllable and self-propelling flow that is sealed from outside influences. Supply chains are rarely like this; for example, external influences can disrupt plans and expectations for the supply chain. Additionally, as will be seen later, linear supply chain thinking can be very limiting and restrictive.

Concurrent with the above changes and developments, have also been changes to general business approaches and technology. The following table shows these changes:

	'Steady as we go' approaches	'Lets go, get ready' approaches
Business	Individual business process decision making Fixed organisational structures Steady and slow economic growth Long product life cycles Passive with at best, reactive management Fixed costs	Collaborative integrated fluid approaches Dynamic and changing flexible structures Unpredictable growth 'Fashion' and shorter product life cycles Proactive management Variable costs
Technology	Standards IT systems Labour intensive Users adapt to the technology	Open integrated systems Automated and self-managing Technology adapts to users

Benefits of supply chain management

Competition in business is not just concerned with companies competing against each other, but also increasingly comes from competing supply chains. Competitive advantage is found by doing things better (service differentiation) or by doing things cheaper (cost leadership) as shown in the following:

Cost leadership	Service differentiation
Standard products produced cheaply	Customer designed products
Production push	Market pull
Flow and mass volume production, with high mechanisation	Job shop production with low mechanisation
Low inventory	Flexible and varied inventory
Focus on productivity	Focus on creativity
Stable planning	Flexible planning
Centralisation	Decentralisation
Standardisation	Bespoke and one-offs

Consider, for example, how Nissans UK synchronised supply chain differs from the supply chains of some other UK car assemblers and ask, which one competes better?

Nissan has adopted a collaborative approach with suppliers, and companies do this for a combination of reasons. Serious threats from the competition or a decline in the markets perhaps have highlighted major problems that have forced change. New initiatives such as 'quality improvement programmes' and 'just in time' have created the need for communicative and problem-sharing relationships.

They need or desire to be in a position to take pre-emptive action rather than simply react with fire-fighting methods.

For example, in the 1980s UK motor manufacturers faced the threat of competition from Europe, the Far East and the USA. After analysing these sources, they had no doubt that the most serious threat for the future was to come from Japan.

They found that the relationship of Japanese motor manufacturers to their suppliers was entirely different from their own:

- There were fewer suppliers and therefore the portfolio was easier and less costly to manage.
- The relationships were very close in that problems were discussed openly and solved together. The technical expertise of suppliers was recognised and they worked with the manufacturers on new designs.
- Suppliers were totally committed to their customers' objectives and were able to identify improvements that their customers could make as well as the buyer identifying changes required at suppliers.

At first, it seemed that the answer lay in the fact that Japanese manufacturers owned many of their suppliers and therefore vertical integration would solve the relationship problem. But when the motor manufacturers examined the relationship in the portions of the supply chain they already owned in the UK, they found just as many, if not more, problems as with external suppliers. Owning a supplier did not improve the relationship in the UK environment. From then on, they knew they had to work towards the concept of collaborating with suppliers and use an approach that would also maximise benefits from the supply chain beyond the first level suppliers.

Looking for these advantages extends from within a company towards its supply chains. This will involve looking to remove sub-functional conflicts from all the interdependent processes; these processes being internal or external to a business. Accordingly, it is the supply chain that now provides a major competitive advantage for a business. This will mean taking a different supply chain approach so that examination is made of the total costs of all the functions matched to the service levels. If this is not done (and by continuing to minimise the costs for each sub-function) this could mean:

- buying in bulk from multiple sources (purchasing is only being optimised), but for example this will give high storage costs;
- making few products with long production runs (here production is only being optimised), which means limited ranges, poor availability, and so on;
- moving in bulk (transport only being optimised), but gives infrequent delivery and so on;
- selling what is produced (marketing only being optimised), but it may not be needed.

The way the supply chain is structured and managed is therefore critical and some reported benefits of adopting a supply chain approach are described below (based on: *Signals of Performance*, The Performance Measurement Group, 2003). It will be noted that different approaches give different results and that the figures give hard evidence that collaborative SCM works.

	No supply chain: functional silos	Internal integrated supply chain	Plus, external integration to the first level only
Inventory days of supply (indexed)	100	78	62
Inventory carrying cost (% sales)	3.2 %	2.1 %	1.5 %
On-time in-full deliveries	80 %	91 %	95 %
Profit (% sales)	8 %	11 %	14 %

It will be seen that with a supply chain approach, inventory costs fall with profit and the service fulfilment increasing, producing the best of both worlds for the companies involved in the approach.

Additional benefits of SCM will only come when there is an examination of all costs/service levels together with all the players. This should produce reduced lead times and improved total costs/service for all parties in the network. This will mean, therefore, going beyond the first tier of suppliers and looking also at the supplier's supplier and so on. It represents more than sharing data and processes: it includes mutual interest, open relationships and sharing. The optimum and the ideal cost/service balance will only ever be found by working and collaborating fully with all players in the supply chain.

A key area here is to balance the service aspects with the costs. Whilst individual companies will need to assess costs for themselves, it can be expected that between 30 and 70 per cent of business cost will be in the supply chain; indeed, cost is a common language to anyone in the supply chain. Managing efficiently and effectively the flows of goods and information across the supply chain networks is therefore essential in bringing about the cost/service balance; a big promise and never an easy approach but resulting in the perfect ideals of:

- increased/improved service, reaction times, product availability and so on;
- reduced/improved total cost, total stock levels, time to market and so on.

Five key aspects for supply chain management

One starting point to developing a better understanding is by mapping a supply chain. This will identify the many parts/players/participants that are involved beyond the first-level contacts. Process mapping covers different techniques ranging from simple flow charts to value stream maps and beyond. Process mapping can be a complex process and one that may usefully be led by external consultants and advisors. Even simple approaches however, are usually very revealing, for example:

1. Determine the company units involved.
2. Agree steps with the people doing the work.
3. Identify the start and end of each process.
4. Go to the next upstream and downstream processes and repeat 1–3.
5. Lay out all the step processes in a flow chart.
6. Insert the lead times between and within each process.
7. Carry on, until all upstream and downstream processes are identified.

This mapping can also be used to ask all the supply chain players what they want, what they buy, their experiences at the pre-order/order and post-order stages, and to use all this information as the basis for improvements.

Meanwhile by having a record of the current processes with the lead times, the next natural step is to critically examine the lead times.

KEY ASPECT 1: LEAD TIME

Lead time is perhaps the critical component in SCM; however, it is usually viewed incrementally and sub-optimally.

Just as time is cash, and cash flow is important to a business, so the associated flows of goods and information that have generated the cash flow in the first place are also important. The cash-to-cash cycle time (C2C) is at the root of cash flow and reducing the time from buying to the receipt of payment for sales is therefore critical.

What follows is a basic view of lead time covering all the elements involved: first, by looking at the eight types of lead time; then followed by an analysis of the component parts of these eight types.

Eight types of lead time

Lead time	Action	By
Pre-order planning	User	Customer
Procurement	Order placing	Customer to supplier
Supplier	Order despatching	Supplier
Production	Making to order	Supplier
Warehouse	Supplying from stock	Supplier
Transit	Transporting	Supplier
Receivers	Receiving	Customer
Payment	Paying	Customer to supplier

Component parts of lead times

Lead time	Lead time stage	Steps, by time
Pre-order planning	User need	Analysing status to determining need to order
	User requisition	Need to order to date of order requisition
Procurement	Order preparation	Order requisition to order release date
	Order confirmation	Order release to date of confirmation
Supplier * see also the production and warehouse lead times	All the stages here are in the following production and warehouse lead times	Confirmation to order despatched date
Production (for example, made to order)	Order processing	Date of order receipt to date order accepted/confirmed
	Preparation	Order accepted to date manufacture starts
	Manufacture (queue time, set up, machine/operator time, inspect/put away times)	Start of manufacture to date it finishes
	Pack/load (to warehouse or to transit LT)	Finished manufacture to date order despatched
Warehouse (for example, available ex stock)	In stock	Date goods arrived to date of order receipt
	Order processing	Order receipt to date order is accepted or confirmed
	Picking	Date order accepted to date order is available/ picked
	Pack/load (to warehouse or to Transit LT)	Order available to date order despatched
Transit		Date despatched to date order received
Receiving		Date order received to date available for issue/use
Payment	Credit	Date invoice received or of other trigger to date payment received
	Payment processing	Date payment received to date cash available for use

Supply lead time

The supply lead time (SLT) used in inventory management should not be confused with the above mentioned supplier lead time. The supply lead time is actually the total of all the above lead times, excluding the payment lead times. Effectively therefore the supply lead time is from the pre-order planning lead time (from analysing the order status/determining the need to order), right through all the above steps and stages to the receiving lead time (date order received to date available for use/issue). It involves many different parties internally in a business and also externally, including both the supplier and the customer.

Lead time examination

Lead times must be examined using real examples, whilst ensuring that all appropriate stages and steps are included. There may also be additional lead times for some players; for example with imports, the customs clearance lead-time.

An example below, using chocolate confectionery, shows some abbreviated results found on lead times:

- supply lead time (cocoa): 180 days on average (once per year crop) with a company in-stock lead time of 70 days (traders are also holding some external stocks);
- supply lead time (ingredients): for example, with nuts 80 days on average (range 10–120 days) and the in-stock lead time of 80 days maximum;
- supply lead time (sugar) 1–2 days with in-stock lead time of 2 days;
- supply lead time (packaging): 1–3 days with in-stock lead time of 3 days maximum;
- production lead time: 1–2 days but product line batch scheduling can mean waiting for 30 days before the next production run;
- warehouse and transit lead times (distribution): 1–5 days with in-stock lead time of 30 days minimum to cover for the production lead time.

After each lead time stage has been quantified, analysis will show if there is a way to do things better. It can be expected that many reductions in lead times will come from the optimising of information flows and not from the goods flows. For example, ICT can rapidly transfer to suppliers the end user demand of a customer and bypass all the customer's internal organisation departments. This will give immediate visibility of requirements to the supplier, enabling them to make decisions in real time and not be less subject to processing delays.

Lead time variability

A crucial aspect when examining lead time is variability. When lead times are realistically looked at, then a range of times will be found; for example from 2 to 8 days. This range represents the variability of lead time. Average calculations are of little practical assistance and can be dangerous if used for planning and decision making.

It is this variability that so often represents the uncertainty found in the supply chain. This is traditionally dealt with by holding safety stocks to cover against the uncertainty.

The variability must, however, be examined by all those involved. Then the variability and the uncertainty can be targeted for replacement with fixed and known and reliable lead times.

The problem of lead variability can be illustrated as follows:

If lead time (LT) is halved from 12 to 6 weeks and lead time variability (LTV) stays the same at + 4 weeks, then:

	Current LT				*New LT*	
LTV	*LT*	*LTV*		*LTV*	*LT*	*LTV*
-4	*12*	*+4*		*-4*	*6*	*+4*

Total LT = 8 to 16 weeks   *Total LT = 2 to 10 weeks*

(Index 100 to 200)   *(Index 100 to 500)*

So, if LTV stays the same, then there is higher disruption/cost and reduced speed (index of 1 to 2 from 1 to 5).

The following are some ways to consider reducing lead time variability:

- demand LTV:
    - predictable known orders/size/make-up;
    - predictable order times;
    - data accuracy on what customers want/when/price;
    - is it the real end users' demand or has it been institutionalised by passing through and influenced by internal and or external supply chain players who do not communicate with each other efficiently?

- supply LTV:
    - predictable known LT;
    - get correct quantity first time;
    - get correct quality first time;
    - data accuracy on what is supplied/price.

The importance of lead time variability in inventory can be seen in the expression, 'Uncertainty is the mother of inventory.' The length of lead time is of secondary importance to the variability and uncertainty in the lead time. Fixed reliable lead times are more important than the length of the lead time.

KEY ASPECT 2: CUSTOMER SERVICE

This is commonly measured by the following on-time, in-full (OTIF) measurements:

- cycle lead time: for example, daily delivery service, order day 1 for day 2 delivery;
- stock availability: for example, 95 per cent of orders are met from stock;
- consistency/reliability: for example, 95 per cent of orders are delivered within three days.

Actual achievement in companies varies; the following may be helpful for comparison purposes:

Key performance indicators – average figures from UK manufacturers

Industry sector	On-time delivery reliability	In-full ex-stock availability	Stock turns per annum
Process	91.0%	97.5%	14
Engineering	92.0%	96.0%	13
Electrical	96.0%	98.2%	9
Consumer household	98.1%	99.0%	21

(*Source*: Best Factory Awards 2001)
(These stock turns figures can be misleading. These are calculated from financial annual accounts by dividing the sales turnover by the value of the stock assets on hand to give an average yearly figure of stock turn.)

Customer importance

It is only the order from the customer that triggers all the activity in the supply chain. Without a customer order, then no supply chain activity is required. The customer is also only interested in buying delivered products.

Customer service levels are a variable and each customer service variable has a cost associated with it. The relationship between cost and service is rarely linear, but more of an exponential curve. So for example, a 10 per cent increase in service may mean a cost increase of 15 or over 50 per cent. Other examples are available from transport: we pay more for first-class mail than for second-class mail; we pay more for a service offering an overnight parcel delivery than for a three-day or a deferred delivery.

Customer value

Customers will place a value on many aspects of the total service offering. Value is placed by customers primarily against delivery/availability but also against quality, cycle lead time, cost and service levels. As perception equates to reality, different customers might see these as being interrelated or may view them independently. It is therefore important for a business to understand the specific reality as seen by the customer. The following are the criteria that customer's value.

Quality is 'performing right first time every time' and involves:

* meeting requirements;
* fitness for purpose;
* minimum variance;
* elimination of waste;
* continuous improvement culture.

Service is concerned with continually meeting customer needs as the market changes and involves:

- support available;
- product availability;
- flexibility;
- reliability;
- consistency.

Cost is knowing what the costs really are and then looking at how to reduce them, and involves:

- design of product;
- manufacturing process;
- distribution process;
- administration process;
- stock levels.

Cycle lead time is about knowing what the lead times really are and then looking for ways to reduce them, and involves considering:

- time to market;
- time from order placement to time available for issue;
- response to market forces.

Quality, cost, service and lead time are all interlinked and customer value can therefore be seen as:

> Increasing **Quality** multiplied by **Service**
> Reducing **Cost** multiplied by **Lead time**

A business therefore, ideally will try to improve the quality and the service, whilst reducing the cost and lead times. All of the aspects are interrelated and connected and it matters not to the majority of customers where the goods come from or whether the goods are transported by road, rail, sea, air and so on. They buy delivered goods.

Who is the customer?

The customer is the reason for the business continually working; to serve the customer better is critical. Thinking has to start from the customer end and must work back into companies. The customer is the business, after all.

But who is the customer? The traditional view is perhaps 'the one that pays the invoices'. But by seeing the customer as 'the next person/process/operation in the chain', then there may well be hundreds of supplier/customer relationships in a single supply chain. If all these single relationships were being viewed as supplier/customer ones, then the whole would be very different. The customers are the business; it is their demand that drives the whole supply chain. Finding out what customers value and then delivering it, is therefore critical.

KEY ASPECT 3: ADDING VALUE

This has become common language in business, but is often confused in meaning. For us, there are two different views:

1. Value is found when something satisfies a need, conforms to expectations and/or gives 'pride of ownership', that is, it is valued over something that is not.

   Here the perception of value will differ. Customers have different perceptions of 'worth' and 'price'. For example, different customers have different perceptions of quality/lead time and the cost/service balance. Maybe therefore, value can be seen as the balance and the pivot point between worth and price or between quality/lead time and cost/service?

2. Value is the opposite to cost and in most processes, more time is actually spent on adding cost and not on adding value, for example:

   - in manufacturing:
     85 per cent of time = queuing/setting up/inspecting/storing and handling = cost adding
     15per cent of time = processing /QA = value adding
   - in warehousing:
     30 days in storage (cost adding) yet only 1 day to pick/pack/load/transit to the customer (value adding)

A business will not find it worthwhile to invest in and automate wasteful non-value-added activities. Waste is the symptom rather than the root cause of the problem, so the aim must be to investigate the cause and then remove the wasteful non-value adders – those processes that take time and resources without adding any value.

   Attention should therefore be given to those activities that do add 'real' value, for example:

   - Make it faster   through   form changes
   - Move it faster   through   time changes
   - Get paid faster   through   place changes

Some examples of adding value in supply chains are:

From	To
Forecasting	Make to order
Inventory push and stock holding	Inventory pull from order placing
Storing	Sorting
Handling	Postponement
Manual ordering	Automated ordering

A supply chain view of added value would also recognise that it is only the movement to the customer that is adding (the ultimate) value. Stopping or delaying the flow adds costs, as shown in Figure 1.3.

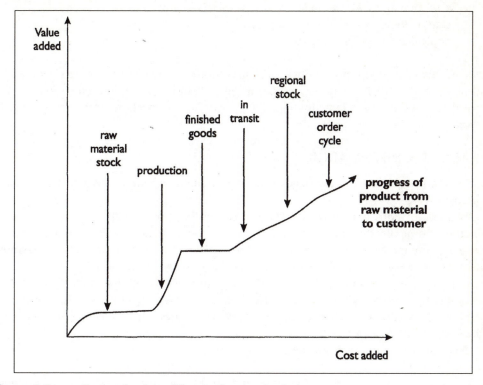

Figure 1.3   Cost and value adders in the supply chain
(*Source*: Cheltenham Tutorial College)

This diagram shows that goods being stored are incurring cost and are not adding value. Whilst this will generally be the case, if those goods being stored were appreciating in value, then this would not apply. This would however only apply for a very limited range of products, such as with bullion (in non-inflation times) and with works of art.

The diagram emphasises that movement to the customer as quickly as possible whilst accounting for the associated cost levels is all that really counts in adding value. Smooth continuous flow movements are preferable and until the value gets to the customer, everything else can be seen as a failure; value only happens with the customer.

KEY ASPECT 4: TRADE-OFFS

This involves looking more holistically with all players across the supply chain(s) and examining the total cost/service balance.

Trade-offs are possible in three basic ways:

- within functions, for example:
  - cost vs. product quality;
  - cost vs. product availability;
- between functions, for example:

- price vs. total acquisition cost (examined later in 'Supply chain operations – purchasing');
- stock vs. JIT supply;
- between companies, for example:
  - transactional vs. collaborative supply;
  - dependable vs. ad hoc supply.

There are therefore many possibilities and opportunities available to integrate/coordinate/ control across the supply chain networks, starting by 'winning the home games first' in and between the internal functions, followed by all external connections to the supply chain networks.

KEY ASPECT 5: INFORMATION

Information is required for every stage of the supply chain and for all levels of supply chain planning.

Advances in both operating systems and computing power make it easier and more economical to obtain this information. ICT enables the collection, analysis and evaluation of data and the transfer of information from one point to another. It attempts to maximise coherent messages and minimise the coupling problems between players.

All parts of the supply chain rely on ICT in planning, operational, administrative and management processes. The customer interface can now be replaced by electronic means.

Information can be used and transferred by techniques which rely on the electronic gathering and manipulation of data.

Electronic communication enables:

- automatic generation of performance monitoring against pre-set key performance indicators;
- automatic tracking of vehicles and loads using global positioning satellites giving constant visibility, improved safety, security and responsive routing and scheduling;
- automatic decision making, for example stock re-ordering against pre-set levels and quantities;
- proposed changes to networks can be modelled so that the effects can be assessed and decisions made.

Data interchange is the transfer of data from one computer to another by electronic means and electronic data interchange (EDI) uses agreed standards in dedicated 'closed' networks; it has been replaced in many applications by 'open' networks of the Web and Internet.

The types of data that can be transferred are:

- trade data, for example quotations, purchase orders;
- technical data, for example product specifications;
- query response, for example order progressing;
- monetary data, for example electronic payment of invoices, electronic ticketing;
- consignment details, for example manifests and customs details.

The use of EDI in the supply chain enables a buyer to have a direct closed network link with a number of its suppliers throughout the supply chain normally referred to as a 'hub'.

Data interchange contributes to shorter lead times and lower stocks. It also enables load manifests and customs data to be transmitted ahead of the shipment, reducing delays in clearing through the import/export process.

Enterprise resource planning (ERP) systems automate the tasks of the major functional areas of an organisation (finance, HR, sales, production, purchasing and distribution) and store all the data from those different areas in a single database, which is accessible by all.

Automatic planning and scheduling (APS) is generally a module of an ERP or material requirements planning (MRP) system, which gathers and analyses data on sales, purchases, production and inventory to ensure that the right materials required for the production process are always available at the right time.

Warehouse management systems (WMS) provide electronic information concurrent with goods movement and integrate physical operations with ERP systems. WMS allows for the handling of higher volumes and can also ease the transition from fixed to random storage positioning.

Automatic identification of inventory is a feature of inventory management systems and facilitates the stock control through devices such as bar coding and radio frequency identification (RFID).

Computer controlled systems are used in storage systems (for example, conveyors) and remote-controlled materials handling equipment (MHE).

Computerised routing and scheduling – routing of transport services can be calculated automatically according to shortest route, quickest route or any variables chosen. Multi-drop operations can be scheduled to give the optimum sequence of pick-ups and drops according to the information provided.

Modelling planners use computer programs to predict flows through new and modified networks and to assess proposals in terms of cost and benefit.

E-business

Electronic business refers generally to commercial transactions that are based upon the processing and transmission of digitised data, including text, sound and visual images, that are carried out over open networks (like the Internet) or closed networks that have a gateway onto an open network (extranet).

E-business is a form of EDI but it uses open, as opposed to closed, networks. Some of the e-business applications are as follows:

- Business-to-business trading exchanges provide a two-way online link between buyers and suppliers; they are now often referred to as a 'marketplace'. Suppliers can advertise their products and services through electronic catalogues; buyers can order from supplier catalogues, take part in auctions, or conduct tendering online; buyers can book travel. In industries with large numbers of buyers and suppliers, third parties generally organise and manage such online forums. In industries with few buyers and a large number of sellers, the buyers often own and run the markets.

- Individual consumers and any system user can get up to-the-minute information, make enquiries, place orders and make payments online. Information about the current position and status of orders services can also be obtained.

Some examples of e-business follow:

Supply chain aspect	Buying	Ordering	Designing products	Post sales
Information	Sharing with suppliers	Visibility	Sharing with suppliers	Customer use records
Planning	Coordinating when to replenish	Forecast sharing/ agreements	New product launching	Service planning
Product flow	Paperless exchanges	Automated	Product changes	Automatic replacement of parts
KPIs	Compliance monitoring	Logistics track and trace	Project monitoring	Performance measurement
Business changes from 'E'	Online auctions, market exchanges	Click on ordering	Mass customisation	Remote sensing and diagnostics, download upgrades

Information is required therefore for every stage of the supply chain and for all levels of supply chain planning.

All parts of the supply chain rely on ICT in the planning, operational, administrative and management processes. It is information flows that lubricate the supply chain; using appropriate ICT is therefore critical.

Approaches to supply chain management

There are three principal approaches to managing supply chains:

- the value chain view
- the Theory of Constraints view
- the lean/agile view.

VALUE CHAIN VIEW

Some observers take the view of the supply chain representing a 'value chain'. Michael Porter of Harvard Business School introduced this concept in 1985 in his book *Gaining Competitive Advantage*. From Figure 1.4, you will see this has large implications for the supply chain. This divides into primary and support activities as follows:

- Primary activities:
    - inbound logistics: stores, warehousing, handling and stock control;
    - operations: production and packing and all activities that transfer inputs into outputs;
    - outbound logistics: transport and warehouse networks to get products to customers;

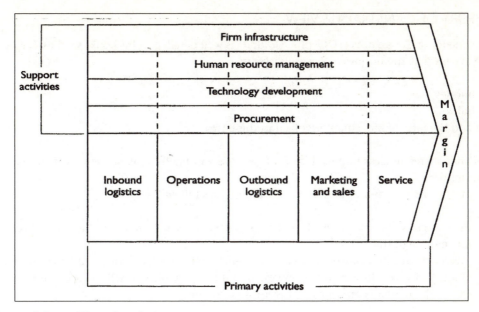

Figure 1.4 The value chain
(*Source*: Cheltenham Tutorial College)

- — marketing and sales: the methods by which customers know about and purchase products;
  - — service: support for all activities such as installation and returns.
- Support activities:
  - — procurement: buying and purchasing of products as well as all other resources;
  - — technology: ICT and R&D;
  - — human resource management: all aspects concerned with personnel;
  - — infrastructure: finance, legal and other general management activities.

Porter then expanded this concept of a value chain into a 'value system'. This consists of a series of linked value chains. By this joining together of value chains into a value system, in effect we create a supply chain. Where the value actually is, according to Porter, is dependant on the way that a customer uses the product and not just on the costs incurred in buying, making and moving it. These costs including all the raw materials and activities that create the product, which then represent its value. But it is only when the product is purchased that the value can be measured and it is not until the product is at the final customer/consumer that the real value is to be found.

Part of the difficulty here, in reality, is that each individual organisation in the supply chain will attempt to define value themselves by looking at their own profitability. Each company will in turn carry on this definition to their suppliers and as the value definition moves back up the chain, then it will become distorted. Indeed, one important reason for companies to try to work together more closely with suppliers and customers is to have a constant view of value throughout the supply/value chain.

THEORY OF CONSTRAINTS VIEW

The Theory of Constraints (TOC) of E. Goldratt is well detailed in his books such as *The Goal*. TOC views that any business is basically about:

- money
- sales
- and the rates of movement involved in these two.

TOC has therefore clear implications for SCM. We will briefly look at some of its important contributions.

TOC views that money and sales are connected as follows:

- throughput – the rate at which money is generated by sales (and by the time it taken to move through the system);
- inventory – the purchase of things that are held to maintain the throughout and the holding of finished goods. It is the money invested in things, intended to sell/awaiting sales;
- costs – the money spent, turning inventory into sales.

TOC notes that how these connections are viewed has now changed, for example:

	Throughput	Inventory	Cost
Past view	Second	Third	First 'The cost world'
View needed now	First 'The throughput world'	Second	Third

This is an interesting perspective as it clearly reverses the view held by those companies who only concentrate on cost control and marginalise all the other aspects.

The importance however, of 'more than cost' perspectives is well supported by many recent approaches in SCM that emphasise, for example, that variable customer service comes from varied rates of throughput and movement. These are the critical aspects that are, refreshingly, included in the 'throughput world' of TOC.

Similarly, procurement approaches that concentrate on total cost of ownership/whole life costs/total acquisition cost all attempt to look wider than just superficial cost aspects.

It can also be seen, that in the traditional input/output diagram of a business, we have the following in Figure 1.5:

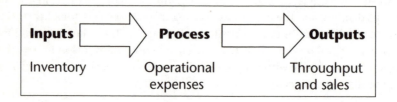

Figure 1.5   Traditional input/output diagram

The money flows can also be seen as follows in Figure 1.6:

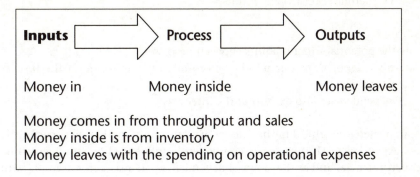

Money comes in from throughput and sales
Money inside is from inventory
Money leaves with the spending on operational expenses

Figure 1.6   Money flows

Putting the above together indicates that the aim of SCM is to:

*   reduce inventory (and reduce the money tied up internally);
*   reduce operational expenses (and reduce the money leaving the company);
*   increase sales/throughout (and increase the money coming into the company);
*   do all the above, at the same time and in balance.

This of course is not always going to be easy, especially when dealing with processes that are being independently managed and have opposing objectives and conflicts between the processes. A better overall total process management may be needed, as a process is a sequence of dependent events, involving time, which has a valued result for the eventual end user.

Processes are selected portions of larger streams of activity that can be transformational (for example, in converting inputs to outputs) and can be transactional (for example, in exchanging outputs for new inputs).

The three key features of processes therefore are dependencies, variabilities and interfaces. Looking at each of these in turn we can see:

*   Dependence:
    —   is sequential and related (knock-on effects);
    —   receives inputs and changes them to outputs;
    —   what happens 'here', causes events 'there';
    — x often needs to be finished, before y can start;
    —   any process will be as efficient as its most inefficient part (a chain is as strong as its weakest link);
    —   the most important factor is, therefore, the most limiting one.

*   Variability:
    —   displays statistical influences (for example, a normal distribution curve), which is especially found with lead times;
    —   is when the 'fixed, known and expected' can become 'variable, unknown and unexpected';
    —   can causes changes from a state of certainty to uncertainty;

—   causes knock-on effects when each part of the process has variability to other processes, with sometimes catastrophic results.

*   Interfaces:
    —   are the potential friction points between processes;
    —   are often ignored, as our minds concentrate on the 'inside of the box' and what happens there;
    —   real dependencies also exist in/at the interface.

Throughput is therefore critical in the Theory of Constraints and is seen occurring at the rate of the last dependency. Throughput is consequently influenced by the fluctuating rates of the other dependencies and as the chain of dependencies increases (for example with long or variable/unreliable supply lead times), then there are going to be:

*   increases in inventory;
*   increases in operating expenses (for example, from the holding/carrying costs of inventory);
*   decreases in throughput (for example, the movement slows).

LEAN AND AGILE VIEW

Lean represents efficiency and eliminating waste by enhancing the flow between source and user to satisfy a known and predictable demand; for example, using MRP and JIT in car manufacturing, where suppliers are selected for product quality and reliability as well as cost.

In the car industry, it can be seen as concentrating more on the supply chain, with 'stock push'. Planning and forecasting can be the main driver, with economic batch quantities and make-to-stock production methods. It takes up to 18 hours to build a new car, yet up to three months to get the car to consumer. (The best producer takes an average of 1.3 months.) These post-production times are being targeted by the car industry under 'the three-day car' banner – this being the lead time from build to the consumer.

Lean can be seen as the response to dealing with the perceived uncertainty in demand; therefore efficient supply management is undertaken. It is the supply side that is lean; the demand side may, however, be 'fat'.

Agile is where demand can be difficult to predict and where there is a need to have a rapid response to the end-market demand. Demand drives the supply chain, for example as in 'efficient consumer response' (ECR) in food retailing where suppliers are selected on speed and flexibility as well as cost.

Food retailers can be seen as concentrating more on the demand chain (or pipeline) with 'demand pull'. The end marketplace (the consumer) is the ultimate demand driver. Therefore with such certainty, this can enable 'make to order' (MTO) and 'assemble to order' (ATO) production. Everything that is bought, produced, moved and handled is in response to a known customer requirement. In turn, this can also mean having modular product structures with postponement until the latest time possible; for example, customisation, kiting and assembly in distribution centres (DCs).

Lean/agile conclusion

The main change needed to become agile is to get close to the market real-time demand. Then all the other challenges will remain for efficient and effective SCM, such as:

- creating value from the customer's perspective;
- identifying the value stream;
- highlighting non-value-added work;
- sharing information;
- process integration by smoothing the supply/demand chain;
- forming a network of companies who work closely together.

These all remain important challenges and require changes to the past traditional ways of supplying products to markets.

Indeed for the car industry, such challenges are conceptually similar to those initially experienced when they changed to JIT supply from the previous bulk-buying and large stock-holding processes.

The terms need not be mutually exclusive. Within a total supply chain viewpoint, therefore, being lean and agile is both efficient and effective, as both sides of supply and demand respond by pulling to the end-market consumer demands in real time. 'Leagility' has been used to describe the combined lean and agile viewpoints.

Supply chain management changes traditional ways

Many supply chains will need to change so they can fully benefit from taking an SCM approach. From our discussion so far, it is useful therefore to have some brief overviews of what may need to change:

From traditional ways	To new ways
Independence	Integration
Independent of next link	Dependency
Links are protective	End/end visibility
Means uncertainty	More certainty
Unresponsive to change	Quicker response
High cost, low service	High service, lower cost
Fragmented internally	Joined up structures
Blame culture	Gain culture
Competing companies	Competing supply chains

The supplier/customer relationship can also change, for example:

From interfacing	To integrating
Supplier selection	Supplier collaboration
Arm's length	Total commitment
Confrontation and power based	Cooperation/collaboration
Day-to-day short term	Year to year and beyond
Clear cut ordering	EDI/visibility
Transactional	Partnership/collaboration
Separated culture	Aligned cultures
Little trust	Extensive trust
Inspect and penalise	Quality assured

In turn this may mean changes in the following aspects:

Aspect	From	To	Means
Order lot size	Large Less frequent orders	Small More frequent orders	Reduced order quantities
Suppliers	Multi-sourcing Short contract Transactional Rejects Low price Arm's length	Single sourcing Long-term contracts No defects Quality Total acquisition cost Collaboration	Fewer suppliers Lower costs Shared developments
Scheduling	Suppliers	Buyers	Less variability
Lead times	Long	Shorter	Less stocks

In turn, this may also mean shifts in organisational buying behaviour.

Organisational buying behaviour has been dramatically changing since the 1970s for at least four reasons:

- First, global competitiveness, especially in the manufacturing sector, such as process machinery, automobiles and heavy engineering, have pointed out the competitive advantages of creating and managing supply chain relationships.
- Second, emergence of the total quality management (TQM) philosophy has encouraged 'reverse marketing' starting with external customers and moving backward into procurement processes and practices, especially as they relate to reduced cycle times and zero inventory management. Also, the TQM philosophy highlights long-term perspectives (for example, transaction orientation). For example, demand-driven manufacturing or flexible manufacturing and operations have been instituted to serve the diversity of demand with respect to form, place and time value to customers over the long term.

- Third, industry restructuring through mergers, acquisitions and alliances on a global basis has reorganised the procurement function from a decentralised administrative function to a centralised strategic function. This is further intensified by outsourcing (buy vs. make) many support functions, such as data processing and human resources.
- Finally, use of information technologies including networked computing, quick response, electronic data interchange and other computer-programmed procurement methods have restructured the buying philosophy, processes and platforms.

WHAT DO SUPPLIERS AND CUSTOMERS WANT?

If we were to simply view what the supplier and the customer wants, then we can see the following position:

Criteria	Suppliers want:	Customers want:
Orders	The business	Delivered/available goods/ services that satisfy a requirement
Information	Clear requirements	Wants clear status information
Performance	Feedback (KPIs that are jointly measured and, benchmarked with other suppliers)	'Feed-forward' (Pre-advice and proactive status/alerts)
Relationship approach	Fairness Involvement/'Part of'	Relationships may be a reflection of the procurement portfolio
Price/cost	Fair	The best total acquisition cost (TAC), total cost of ownership (TCO), life cycle cost (LCC), whole life cost (WLC)
Quality	Clarity on what it means and what is valued by the customer	Fit for purpose
Delivery	On time, in full (OTIF)	OTIF
Quantity	Large regular orders	Smaller, frequent deliveries
Time	Supplier lead time	Supply lead time
Place	Ex-works (international) or Factory gate pricing (domestic trade)	Delivered domicile duty paid or Delivered/carriage paid
Payment time	Prompt	To negotiate

This indicates the so-called 'opposite' and the 'them/us' scenarios. However, it also indicates that there are some very common wants:

- Orders are the fundamental reason for the relationship as it is the order that drives the supply chain. Customers who are very clear on their specific requirements may generate a response from their suppliers that gives alternative options. Sharing of requirements is useful; after all, suppliers 'do not know what they do not know'.

- Information is another common objective involving two-way communications that gives mutual understanding.

- Performance is another two-way process with feedback to suppliers on performance and feed-forward from suppliers to customers with order status reports and pre-alerts on problems. For example, the supplier advising of a delay at least enables the customer to plan; it also builds up trust, understanding and removes uncertainty. Why, for example, should customers need to expedite?

- Relationships: well this is the major part of this book to be covered later, so there is no summary here!

- Price/cost: if total cost-of-ownership evaluation approaches are used, then there is really little to stop the sharing of the results with suppliers. Again, this can mean that they may be able to better suggest alternatives and options. It will also show fairness, which, after all, is what the supplier looks for.

- Quality: clarity and understanding will enable the meeting of requirements.

- Delivery has common measures (for example, OTIF) for both suppliers and customers and if both parties record these on a per transaction basis and then share such measurements openly on a period basis, they will find this enables better communications and understanding. It also will prevent any juvenile 'you did/I did not' debates between suppliers/customers, which will eventually lead to mistrust and feelings that 'they' are unreliable.

- Quantity: the differences in order quantities between the parties will require discussion within the overall negotiations. It may be that allowing supplier's access to demand information and forecasts will enable the suppliers to better plan their production and thus enable the customer requirements for smaller, more frequent deliveries.

- Time: this is interesting one as in principle the supplier lead time can only kick off after the customer's internal process in the total supply lead time. If therefore the eventual users with the customer's company report continual delays in supply, it may not be always the fault of the actual supplier. An examination of the earlier coverage on lead times indicated that all the process involved the lead-time chain and emphasised the need for an overall view.

- Place: here the assumption is that the supplier is only interested in producing/selling a product and that it is the customers' responsibility to come and get it. Meanwhile, the customers may require goods delivered to them including all duties/taxes and so on. Of course it is a fact that to enable full comparisons, goods need to be costed at the place where they are to be consumed/used; again a negotiation point and one where some customers can find advantage in buying from suppliers on ex-works terms as they then get clearer lead-time visibility and control of both the transit lead times and freight/logistics cost prices.

• Payment time: a clear negotiation aspect.

Supply- or demand-led supply chains

The need to work together has been shown both internally and externally to balance the supply with the demand. If this is not done, then demand can be amplified as it passes down the chain and shows the 'Forrester Effect'. (Forrester was a researcher at the US Massachusetts Institute of Technology (MIT) in the late 1960s who observed that small impacts in one area can have large 'knock-on' effects elsewhere. The book *Limits to Growth* written by DH Meadows in 1972 covers this foundational work on system dynamics.)

When applied to supply chains, a four-player supply chain will typically have the following stock levels:

Factory →	Distributor →	Wholesaler →	Retailer
250	245	205	100

Note: these figures represent stock levels, being indexed at 100 with the retailer. So the multiple, for example at the factory end is times 2.5. (The above figures are averaged from over 10 000 computer simulations. Such simulations are available from playing the 'Lego Game' and 'Beer Game'.)

The problem here is that each player works independently from all others and only takes a view of their immediate next-in-line player; each is uncertain on what is going to happen, and therefore covers themselves by holding safety stock.

This increase in stock and the 'bullwhip effect' is explained by Figure 1.7, where it will be seen that each player is holding safety stock as a protection from both the uncertainty in supply and/or demand. The only way to prevent this is by having all the four players integrate, coordinate and control together the supply to match demand as far as possible; for example, if the factory and distributor and wholesaler had visibility of the retailer's end demand, and all were working together collaboratively.

Additionally, such impacts can be found purely internally. Consider for example those internal company users who have no confidence or visibility in their internal order/delivery processes and therefore have squirrel stores that are holding safety stocks. This effect has been shown above in a single supply chain. Imagine the impact on multiple level supply chains and networks?

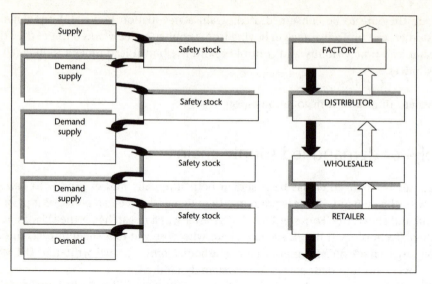

Figure 1.7   'Bullwhip effect'

DEMAND REPLENISHMENT IN NETWORKS

Most players in SCM have multiple levels of supply chain involvements. Therefore, managing inventory in a sequential and simple supply chain is different to that found when having to manage inventory across these multiple-level supply chains, for example within a distribution network or across many different players. The following will show some of differences:

Key area	Simple supply chain	Multiple-level supply chain
Objective for inventory levels	Incremental view per DC/ stock holding place	Total view across the supply chain
Demand forecasts	Independent at each level	Based on end customer
Lead times	Work on first-level supplier's lead time and variability	Use all/holistic lead times
Forrester Effects	Ignored, 'not my problem'	Measured and allowed for in replenishment planning
Visibility	To first-level supplier and customer only	Holistic visibility
Customer service	Differentiation not possible	Differentiation possible
Cost implications	Incremental costs giving high holistic cost levels	Modelled for optimisation across the supply chain

Transactional or collaborative supply chains

Changing from transactional/responsive to collaborative/adaptive supply chains makes an interesting comparison. Another 'ideal-typical' comparison follows:

Transactional	Collaboration
Price/risk	
Price orientation	Total cost of ownership
Price dominates	Shared destiny dominates
One way	Two-way exchanges
Customer demands sensitive data	Exchanges of sensitive data
Customer keeps all cost savings	Mutual efforts to reduce costs, times and waste
All risk with supplier, the buyer risks little	Shared risk and benefits
'What is in it for me?'	'What is in it for us?'
Short term	Long term
Negotiations	
Strong use of ploys in negotiations	Mutual gains 'rule' discussions
Power based	Equality based
Win/lose	Win/win
'One-off' deals	'For ever' together
'One night stand'	'Marriage'
Walk in and out, change is easy	Difficult to break, change is difficult
Easy to set up	Difficult to set up
Adversarial and maybe inefficient for one party	Challenging to implement and continue with
'Partnershaft'	Partnership
Interpersonal relationships	
No personal relationships	Strong personal relationships
Separated/arm's length	Close/alliance
Low contact/closed	Shared vision/open
Predatory power based	Proactive and more people based
Hierarchical/superior subordinate	Equality
Blame culture	Problem-solving 'gain' culture
Alienated employees	Motivated employees
Trust	
Trust is based on what the contract says = contractual trust	Trust is based on goodwill, commitment and cooperation
Little ongoing trust	Continual trust plus risk/benefits sharing
Power-based 'spin'	Pragmatic 'tough' trust
Controls	
Strong on tactical/departmental controls	Strong on marketing strategy and supply chain alignment
High formal controls	Self-controlled
Rigid contracts	Flexible contracts
Technical performance and the specifications 'rule'	Work beyond just 'one' technical view
Resource and capacity capabilities	Mutual long-term capabilities
Measure by non-compliance	Both measure and agree remedial action

The change from transactional methods to collaborative approaches goes far beyond the technical issues of ICT connectivity, and fully embraces the soft skills. If all the supply chain parties would work together then a lot more would get done more efficiently and more effectively. The evidence for this from relationship principles seems overwhelming yet many will not subscribe to a mutually sharing, collaborative SCM approach.

A major reason for this is that business is founded on power, for example, the suppliers' 'anger at unreasonable demands, unsustainable prices and the rejection of high quality produce' by a supermarket company (Bell S). Therefore two-way collaboration can sit here as an uneasy concept; it is easy to beat someone up when you have some power over their business/life. Power here is from the position of the buying company and the control they have of the resources, for example further orders, payments to the supplier. It therefore ignores the power of knowledge that the supplier could contribute to improvements and doing things better.

Another major reason for the lack of two-way collaborative approaches is also that soft skills are the hard skills for many people in business. SCM collaboration between companies will not succeed without appropriate recognition that soft-skill development is required; after all any relationship depends on trust and without trust, there is no relationship.

Meanwhile, for those who are nervous about 'soft and fluffy' approaches and choose to ignore that the soft stuff is really the hard stuff, then will they please consider using the following with any group of people:

- Fill a 500 ml glass with 250 ml of water.
- Show this to the group.
- Ask the question: 'What do you see?'
- The answer will be either: 'The glass is half full,' or, 'the glass is half empty'.

There is a totally opposite difference and meaning in these answers. Yet people have viewed the same thing. This is the soft emotional side and this is the reality when dealing with people. Still from a logical science and hard side, there is no difference in meaning; the glass has 250 ml of water, full stop and finish.

With people, perception is reality and feelings are facts. As has been noted by Peter Drucker, the soft/psychological/feelings part of people is important: 'Finding and realising the potential of a business is psychologically difficult. It will always be opposed from within because it means breaking down old established habits.'

Those who ignore such simple truths are destined to make serious mistakes and have major disappointments. Again very simple to say, yet many do not realise this and if they do, they do not practise it. An important topic we shall return to in the later section on 'Supply chain thinking' (page 119).

Contrasts between Type I and Type II supply chains

The following model for two types of supply chain presents an 'extremes' view to stimulate debate and discussion about the changes that may be needed. This is not intended to be a good or bad comparison. The reality and the practice will be found in the grey between the black/white extremes; also, some aspects can be mixed between the two types. For example Type I on the main drivers and products; but Type II on inventory and buying and so on.

Attribute	Type I supply chain Production led Push More about supply	Type II supply chain Market led Pull More about demand
Main driver	Forecast driven	Order driven
	Growth from volume output and ROI	Growth from customer satisfaction
	Financial performance profit driven	Customer focus, value driven
	'Pump' push	'Turn on the tap' pull
	From supply to demand	From demand to supply
	Mass production	Mass market
Products	Launched	Transition
	Functional, standard, commodities	Innovative, design and build, fashion goods
	Low variety	High variety
	Long product life cycle	Short product life cycles
Inventory	'Turns'	'Spins'
	Stock holding	Little stock holding
	Just in case	Just in time
	Hold safety stock	No safety stock
	Seen as an asset/protection	Seen as a cost and liability
Buying	Buy goods for anticipated and projected demand/needs	Assign capacity on a daily basis
	Instructed suppliers	Involved suppliers
	Arm's length, played off on a short-term basis	Committed suppliers, long-term basis
	Confrontation	Cooperation
	Adversarial	Alliances
	Narrow range of suppliers	Ordered supplier base of specialists
	Low-cost buying	Total acquisition cost buying
	Inspection on receipt	Quality assured
Making	Build	Supply
	Proactive with orders	React to orders
	Economy of scale	Reduce waste
	Continuous flow and mass production	Batch, job shop, project methods of production, 'customising'
	Long runs	Short runs
	Low production costs	Higher production costs
	High work in progress inventory	Low work in progress inventory
	High plant efficiency e.g. 24/7	High effectiveness but with lower plant efficiencies
	Labour is an extension of the machine	Labour brings the continuous improvements
	Ordered 'push' schedules and reliable demand forecasts/make to stock	Flexible 'pull' Kanban schedules with make/assemble to order

Attribute	Type I supply chain Production led Push More about supply	Type II supply chain Market led Pull More about demand
Moving	Move slower in bulk Large/less frequent deliveries Storage is high cost Transport is a low cost Fewer but larger RDC type deliveries	Move faster in smaller quantities Smaller, frequent deliveries Storage is low cost Transport costs are higher Many varied and dispersed destinations
Customers	Predictive demand Cost driven Are only handled at the top or by the customer service department	Unpredictive demand Availability driven Everybody is customer focused
Information	Demand information is sometimes passed back Used mainly for executing	Demand information is mandatory Used also for planning purposes
Handling of Customers orders	10% forecast error and algorithmetic- based forecasts Continuous scheduled replenishment More push Stock outs rarer (1–2%) and are dealt with contractually Stable and consistent orders, some predictable weekly type ordering Clear-cut ordering Service levels are more rigid	40–100% error with forecasts more consultative based Real-time visibility throughout the supply chain More pull Stock outs are immediate and frequent (10–40% pa) and volatile Cyclical demand, many unpredictable orders EDI/visibility ordering Service levels are more flexible to actual forecasts
Deliver from stock lead times	Immediate, fast in one or two days	Immediate to long; slower and from days to weeks
Make to order lead times	1–6 months as mainly making standard products for stock	1–14 days
Costs	Mainly in physical conversion/ movements Inventory costs in finished goods Cost control very strong and any gained savings are retained	Mainly in marketing Inventory costs in raw materials/WIP Revenue generation and any gained savings are shared
Producer selling price	Low selling price Few markdowns 5–20% profits Low risk	Higher selling price Many end of season markdowns 20–60% profits Higher risk levels

Attribute	Type I supply chain Production led Push More about supply	Type II supply chain Market led Pull More about demand
Organisation methods	Silo/hierarchical management with some cells	Flatter structures with cross-functional teams
	Top down to staff gives orders and responsibility	Top down and bottom up giving assistance; everyone is responsible
	Professional managers who are more driven by power	Leaders/educators who are people driven
	Transactional/ownership	Partnership/collaborative
	Self-interest	Customer interest
	Protective interfacing links	Visible integrated links
	Slow to change, change is mainly resisted, and maintenance of the status quo	Quicker response with continuous improvement and more embracive of change
	Internal fragmentation with instructed employees	Joined up structures with involved employees
	Tendency for blame cultures	More gain structure
	'Fire-fighting'	'Fire-lighting'
	Little trust	Extensive trust
	People are a liability and numbers are to be reduced wherever possible	People are an asset to be invested in
	Narrow skill base	Multiple skill bases
	Outside recruitment	Internal recruitment also
	'Do what you are told'	'Do what you think is best'

Supply chain operations

Within each component/functional process of the supply chain (buying, making, moving and selling), specific aspects can be found that will assist in supply chain optimisations. These operations will be examined briefly in this section.

PURCHASING

Before buying any goods or services, fundamental questions to be asked are:

1. Is it needed?
2. Can the need be met in another way?
3. Is it already to be found elsewhere within the company?
4. Can the requirement be met by sharing rather than purchasing?
5. Can the requirement be met by renting rather than by purchasing?
6. Is the quantity required essential?
7. Can it serve any useful purpose after its initial use?
8. Is the value added to the business greater than the total cost of ownership?

Total cost of ownership

This is a philosophy that includes value.

The total cost of ownership (TCO) sees that the benefit of ownership only comes when the value added to the business through owning the asset is greater than the TCO.

Conceptually therefore:

$$TCO \quad = \quad Price$$
$$+$$
$$total\ acquisition\ cost\ (TAC)$$
$$+$$
$$life\ cycle\ costs\ (LCC)\ or\ whole\ life\ costs\ (WLC)$$

Both TAC and WLC are examined below.

Total acquisition cost

This is the price paid plus all the other costs paid by the buyer:

- quality, for example errors, defects, returns;
- delivery, for example modes, time scales;
- delivery performance, for example non-availability, unreliability;
- lead time, for example stock financing;
- packing, for example point of display repacks;
- warehousing, for example extra handling;
- inventory, for example product deterioration;
- new supplier, for example start-ups, assessments, negotiations;
- administration, for example orders processing.

The real question to ask is: what are these other costs?

Whole life costing

This is the same as life cycle costing and can be defined as the systematic consideration of all relevant costs and revenues associated with the acquisition and ownership of the asset and a means of comparing options and their associated cost and revenue over a period of time.

WLC covers:

- initial capital/procurement costs, for example design, construction, installation, purchase, or leasing fees and charges;
- future costs, for example all operating costs (rent, rates, cleaning, inspection, maintenance, repair, placements/renewals, energy, dismantling, disposal, security, and management). Note that unplanned and unexpected maintenance/refurbishment may amount to more than half of the initial capital spent;
- opportunity costs, for example the cost of not having the money available for alternative investments, which would earn money, or the interest payable on loans to finance work.

Purchasing portfolios

These examine the critical aspects to be examined that establish the strategic importance of a product to the business

1 Risk/spend by product and relationship

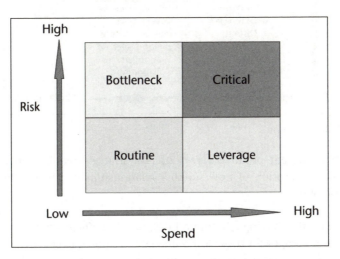

Figure 1.8   Product categories

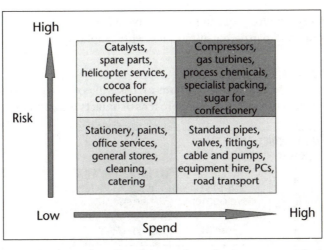

Figure 1.9   Examples from the oil and gas and confectionery manufacturing industries

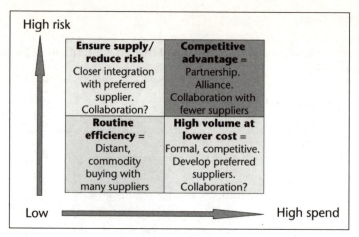

Figure 1.10   Relationships

These indicate that different products have different strategic requirements to a business. It also gives a broad indication of how supplier relationships can be conducted using the following four basic strategies:

- Routine items: routine buying of commodities, needing efficiency. Relationships may be conducted at arm's length for those low-value items required irregularly.
- Critical items: need here is to ensure the supply and reduce the risk.
- Leverage items: a high volume is purchased therefore needing to obtain at the lowest cost.
- Bottleneck/strategic items: requiring competitive advantage. These will involve longer-term relationships and partnering approaches with suppliers.

2   Supplier/buyer power
The balance of power in the four above positions on risk will not be equal. This is shown in the following diagram where the variation in approaches/contacts is again emphasised.

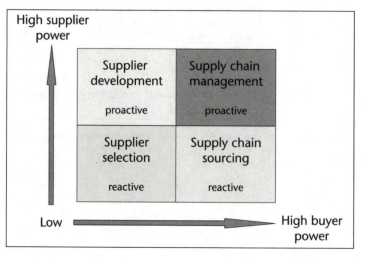

Figure 1.11   Buyer/supplier power

A UK research survey (after Cox et al., *Logistics Europe*, June 2003) found the following breakdown in purchasing:

- 68% = Routine/commodity buying/supplier selection.
- 12% = Bottleneck/reduce risk-preferred supplier/supplier development. Collaboration?
- 13% = Leverage/reduce price-preferred supplier/supply chain sourcing. Collaboration?
- 7% = Critical/competitive advantage-partnerships/supply chain management. Collaboration.

Therefore, varied sourcing approaches are found; it will however be noted that three of them will possibly involve collaboration. The approach of Cox et al. shows that all purchases and relationships are not equal and also shows where most of the transactions take place (that is in routine commodity buying). SCM, as shown above being only involved in one quadrant, conflicts with the commonly held view of SCM. Therefore we have the view that SCM is also involved in the buyer/supplier transactions and relationships of the above supplier selection, development and supply chain sourcing.

World-class purchasing guidelines

- What are the annual spend and requirements of the purchasing portfolios?
- Is there a programme to reduce the procurement lead times?
- Is component variety limited by looking closely at users' specifications (avoiding brand names) and duplicated purchasing?
- What are the supplier assessment methods and supplier management policies?
- Do all communication processes deliver understanding?
- What codification is used?
- Is SCM used?
- Is end-to-end product evaluation used by applying the TCO?
- What programme is there to develop relationships with users/customers and with external suppliers?
- Is there a culture of total quality?
- Have buyers changed from being reactive order placers to be proactive commodity managers?
- Should you outsource or manage procurement yourself?
- Is there a programme to reduce the supplier base to a small number of qualified suppliers fully integrated into the business?
- Is there a culture of continuous improvement?

PRODUCTION

Production and manufacturing in the UK has been relatively late in changing to embrace demand-driven needs for smaller, make-to-order batches. The conflicts between volume and variety are a main consideration in production and traditionally, high volume with low variety (and low price) was seen as the only way. However, changes have been made in those industries that have remained in the UK meanwhile offshoring has been used for much of the former UK manufacturing and production base.

Making to order or making to stock

This is the separation point between forecasting and ordering and gives five positions or 'decoupling points' (DP) as shown in Figure 1.12.

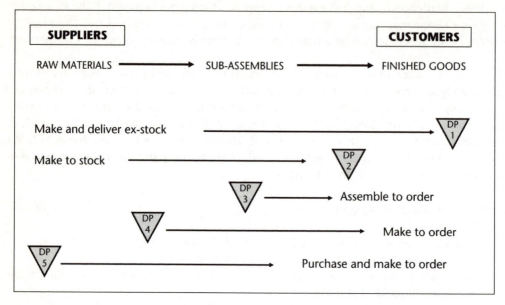

Figure 1.12   Make to order or to stock?

The DP 1–5 positions, separated by forecasts and order activities, are as below:

1. Make and deliver from stock = forecast driven
   Examples are fast-moving food products that are held in regional distribution centres, near to retail outlets.
2. Make to stock (MTS) = forecast driven
   Examples are slower-moving consumer and food items that are held more centrally in central distribution centres.
3. Assemble to order (ATO) = order driven
   Dell PCs, most furniture and beds are examples of this method of production with, increasingly, cars.
4. Make to order (MTO) = order driven
   An example is top of the range cars like a Rolls Royce and specialist PCs.
5. Purchase and make to order = order driven
   High tech and large capital one-off items are examples here, such as ships

From a production aspect, the following can be found:

- DP 1: typically continuous flow production with very high volume produced but with no product variation; such as with petrol and steel.
- DP 2: typically dedicated line flow production with very high volumes made and with little product variation; the mass production of cars was traditionally a good example.

- DP 3: typically mixed product line flow with medium volumes produced of medium product variations; the manufacturing of clothes is an example here as is the 'newer' method now used for car assembly.
- DP 4: typically batch flow production with lower volumes of high product variation; job shops like printers being an example here.
- DP 5: typically job shop production of very low volumes but very high product variations; project one-off item like ships being one example.

These positions give rise to the following supply chain basic options where:

- 'Push' involves forecast-driven activity that pushes and supplies stock towards the customer. Here it is held to await the customers' demand orders. It involves the inventory holding of finished goods and is risky in as much as it is dealing more with uncertainty in demand.
- 'Pull' involves actual demand orders pulling stock through the supply chain from the point of supply. It is responsive directly to these orders and involves the products matching exactly what customers order. It involves the holding stock of semi-finished work in progress or even no inventory at all as certain raw materials can be ordered to specifically manufacture a customer order. There is less risk with this option as nothing is more certain than the customer's order.

Activity	MTS(DP 1/2) 'Make then sell' Supply-demand Forecast demand 'Push' supply	MTO(DP 4/5) 'Sell then make' Demand-supply Order 'Pull' supply
Main driver	Forecasts Structured planning and scheduling	Orders Sense and respond using real-time information
Buying	Is for anticipated needs by instructing suppliers Focus on cost and quality	Is for daily needs using involved suppliers Focus on speed, quality and flexibility
Product	Standardised products Cost driven	Can be bespoke and modular More quality driven
Customer lead time	Fast and short	Slower
Production	Low cost as uses long production run lengths High average utilisation	Higher costs and short run lengths and fast production line changes Excess buffer capacity is used
Inventory	Cost is in finished goods and uses safety stock Stock is viewed as an asset and as a protection	Cost is in raw materials and work in progress with little safety stock Stock is viewed as a liability
Distribution	Storage costs are high with low transport costs (as moving in bulk)	Storage costs are low with transport costs being higher as moving smaller quantities more frequently

The 'make then sell' position is well represented by the Henry Ford expression of 'You can have colour you want, as long it as it is black,' and by the traditional manufacture/assembly of consumer goods. Nowadays, cars for example, follow the 'assemble to order' (position three) that involves assembling a specific order from stocks of components/work in progress. This method of production represents for many the optimum production trade-off in the supply chain as final assembly is only taking place on receipt of the order; the final product production being postponed until an firm order is received. It also means adopting a more challenging form of SCM.

World-class production guidelines

*   Is product delivered on time in full (OTIF) more than 99 per cent of the time?
*   Is there a programme to reduce production lead times?
*   Is material received fit for purpose and supplied to the point of use without inspection?
*   Do all communication processes deliver understanding?
*   Does the layout enable sequential operations?
*   Are set-up times reduced to the minimum?
*   Is SCM used?
*   Are non-value-added costs progressively reduced?
*   Is there a culture of total quality?
*   Is there an active policy to keep areas clean and tidy?
*   Does the product design facilitate production?
*   Is there a culture of continuous improvement?
*   Should you outsource or manage production yourself?

PHYSICAL DISTRIBUTION

Definitions

Definitions can be important to clarify thought especially when one person understands a term to mean one thing, but another person understands the same term differently. This has occurred for example in the UK from the mid-1990s with 'logistics'.

Logistics, which originally encompassed the whole supply chain, is now being understood by many companies as a new name for transport or for warehousing/stores or for distribution. Third-party transport companies are also now beginning to call themselves SCM companies. Logistics can therefore be a confusing word. Additionally, some people use the term logistics to describe their own internal company process, and use the supply chain term, when they are dealing with external suppliers/customers. At the risk of further confusion, others also call their internal logistics processes the internal supply chain.

Physical distribution meanwhile is about delivering the right goods to the right place at the right time and at the right cost. This so-called 'rights of distribution' definition represents in a simple way the objectives for distribution. Distribution therefore involves the combining of transport with warehousing, and is a term that is often applied to mainly finished goods. However, it may also by used by suppliers who are delivering product to their customer, perhaps raw materials and semi-finished work-in-progress goods. Suppliers are also concerned with getting the 'rights' correct and, as far as that supplier is concerned, the raw materials can be for them the finished goods.

Meanwhile, when readers hear the three terms of logistics, supply chain and distribution, they are strongly recommended to ensure they have a proper understanding of what the originator means by the specific word. This can be very important and prevent confusion.

Distribution and the supply chain

Physical distribution is the method by which goods move from one location to another and is an essential function in product supply chains. This movement can be for raw materials, sub-assemblies/work in progress, or for the finished goods over shorter distances on a national basis, or over longer distances and on a global basis.

In demand-driven supply chains, warehouses are mainly used for storing goods or involve more sorting activities; both being required to largely feed external customers. In the supply-driven supply chains, warehouses are known as stores and hold stocks to feed internal activities, like production.

World-class distribution guidelines

The following are the basic points that everyone involved in managing distribution must be alert to.

- Do you need each warehouse in the distribution network?
- Is there a programme to reduce all the distribution lead times?
- How can each item be packed?
- What products should be kept and where?
- Is product delivered on time in full (OTIF) more than 95 per cent of the time?
- Is SCM used?
- How many times are products handled?
- Are products stored in relation to the flow/rate of movement?
- Is the warehouse layout and transport network optimal?
- Is the right transport mode being used?
- What are the operational standards?
- Do we have a multi-skilled workforce?
- Is there a culture of continuous improvement?
- Should we outsource or manage distribution ourself?
- Is there a culture of total quality?

MARKETING

It is customer demand that drives the total supply chain; therefore the marketing process has some useful viewpoints, as has been usefully noted by Peter Drucker:

> Marketing is so basic that it cannot be considered a separate function. It is the whole business seen from the point of view of its final result, that is, from the customers' point of view … Business success is not determined by the producer but by the customer.

It is interesting to observe that marketing, like SCM, has gone thorough many changes in recent years:

Forward marketing 'Old'	Reverse marketing 'New'
Production-led as everyone would buy	Market-led to determine what everyone needs to buy
Design and make the product first	Find out the customer needs and then design the product
High volume, low variety = 'Any colour you want as long as it is black' (Henry Ford)	Customers' needs are known in advance of production
Sell what is produced and promote any unsold goods	Make only what can sell and make to order
Focus on sellers' needs and make to stock	Customer satisfaction and loyalty

Basic tenets of marketing:

- Customers are the basis of the business.
- We need to know who they are and what they need.
- We must anticipate customers' changing needs.
- Everyone in the organisation is involved in marketing.
- We must develop long-term relationships with our customers.

It will be observed that these tenets are the same for demand-led SCM.

The marketing 'Ps'

A cornerstone of a marketing approach are the 'Ps'.

Product/service supplied looks at the following:
- features (physical, service, psychological);
- what it look like;
- what will be delivered;
- description, including benefits;
- value to the customer (what is in it for me?);
- customisation/tailoring.

Place:
- distribution channels – how to get products to the marketplace, for example direct, via wholesalers, via retailers and so on;
- market positioning and competition in the marketplace;
- inventory levels – where and what format to hold;
- physical distribution management – the moving of products to the marketplace;
- Internet marketing and e-shopping.

*P*hysical facilities:
- premises;
- impacts to first time visitor/users;
- stationery/PR material/appearance.

*P*rice:
- cost-plus process, or;
- market nature-/market-based prices;
- competition pricing;
- customer perceptions and expectations.

*P*romotion:
- communications;
- two-way understanding;
- 'the object of communication is to prevent misunderstanding';
- 'the meaning of communication is in its effect';
- moving through stages of unaware–aware–comprehension–conviction–action;
- using negotiation/persuasion.

*P*eople:
- image;
- skills and experiences;
- attitude and behaviour.

Working through the 'Ps' will show the basis of customers' needs, the resultant differentiation required and the supply chain design.

World-class marketing guidelines

- Who are the key customers?
- What differentiates the company from the competition?
- When was the last SWOT (strengths/weaknesses/opportunities/threats) analysis undertaken?
- When was the last PEST (political/economic/social/technological) analysis undertaken?
- Is the marketplace fully understood?
- Is there a culture of total quality? (Quality is examined later in the section 'Supply chain thinking and approaches.)
- What is the market segmentation policy?
- Do customer contact staff have the authority to fully resolve problems?
- Do all communication processes deliver understanding?
- Is the 'time to market' at a minimum?
- Is there a flexible workforce?
- Is there a culture of continuous improvement?
- Is the company a market-driven one?
- Is SCM used?

VIEWPOINT
RESTRUCTURING UK MANUFACTURING SUPPLY CHAINS

1. Restructure capital
    Emphasis has been on short-term growth, which is fashionable in the City. However, long-term investment is needed.

2. Examine and invest in processes
    Examine waste in capital, process standardisation, product portfolio rationalisation and work across the supply chain:
    • get the internal supply chain correct – styles, culture, trust, communication;
    • develop a clear way forward – tangible deliverables, aligned accountabilities, adequate resources;
    • transparency – forecast and performance information with consistent actions;
    • drive by time performance – lengths of time for each process, total time, lead time excesses;
    • add value with the process, not cost;
    • develop reliability for what is out of tolerance.

3. Segment the portfolio
    • view each product as a separate supply chain with varied demands, product characteristics, operational capability, distribution channels, supplier profiles and market dynamics;
    • install effective KPIs to give visibility and to drive action;
    • install internal/customer/supplier relationships at each interface.

4. Invest in product leadership
    Labour-intensive, low-value products are not the way forward – understand costs and trim lower margin products. Value-added products are needed.

5. Develops skills base
    Relying on others to train is not acceptable; this has been the problem from the last 20 years.

6. Know the market
    Market research is needed.

7. Consolidate
    Critical mass is needed, as in automotive and electronics.

(*Source:* Based on a report in *Storage Handling and Distribution*, December 2002)

Problems in integrating supply chains

As will have been seen already, the theory of effective and efficient SCM is relatively clear; it is the application and the practice that is difficult. SCM is classic common sense; but then, whilst it may be sense, it is not very common.

Some of the reasons for this and the problems are due to the following factors:

- inaccurate forecasting of demand;
- volatile markets and demand patterns;
- unwillingness to share information;
- power forcing by large dominant customers;
- resistant monopoly suppliers;
- poor ICT;
- management styles and approaches;
- poor and unreliable delivery performance;
- global/long-distance suppliers and/or markets;
- resistance to change;
- lack of knowledge/resources;
- misunderstanding of how independently managed processes interact.

To further our view of these problems and difficulties, the following viewpoint reflects the wide-ranging views of what is needed to restructure UK manufacturing. The links to SCM principles are very clear and show some of problems and requirements for integrating supply chains.

Supply chain strategy

The strategic aspects are concerned with 'how we will win' and means having an awareness of the expected development of the business in the future:

- product format, volumes and throughputs;
- inventory holding;
- suppliers and purchasing methods;
- production methods;
- physical distribution methods;
- customers and marketing methods.

The strategic direction will be assisted by having a 'mission' for the supply chain.

MISSION/VISION

From our forgoing discussion, it is possible to view that the mission of SCM is to have:

- transparent flows;
- flexibility;
- a share-to-gain approach;
- reliance on quality;
- elimination of all barriers to all the internal and external activities;
- elimination of inventory whilst optimally balancing costs, service levels and availability.

INVENTORY

In the supply chain, the flows of goods and information will need coordinating to minimise inventory levels. Inventory is the common component throughout the supply chain, either as raw material, sub-assemblies/work in progress or as finished goods (which are often held at multiple places in the supply chain). It can also be the 'knock-on' from one player to another player, as seen earlier in the Forrester Effect.

To prevent such effects, 'one number' views at individual stock keeping unit (SKU) levels of the forecasts and orders are required throughout the supply chain. Inventory is therefore an important component to understand and any changes in supply chain structuring will inevitably have impacts on where and how much inventory is being held. As already noted, the format of inventory and where it is held is of common interest to all supply chain players and must be jointly investigated and examined.

Inventory management is an approach to manage the product flow in a supply chain, to achieve the required service level at an acceptable cost. Movement and product flow are key concepts: when the flow stops, then cost will be added (unless the stored product is one that appreciates in value over time).

Key aspects that are to be considered in inventory management are:

* determining the products to stock and the location where they are held;
* maintaining the level of stock needed to satisfy the demand (by forecasting of demand);
* maintaining the supply;
* determining when to order (the timing);
* determining how much to order (the quantity).

Lead time is a critical component in making inventory decisions; as the following simple example illustrates:

If the use is 70 items per week, and the supply LT is 2 weeks, then, the maximum stock is 140 items.

But if the supply LT is variable by +/- one week, then, the maximum stock is 210 items and the minimum stock is 70 items.

People may play it safe and hold 210 items; this is not the best decision but may be an understandable one for those who are left to base replenishment decisions on protecting against personal risk factors when past stock-outs have occurred.

In such cases, then clearly inventory management is neither understood nor involved strategically and operationally in the business.

When making replenishment decisions, the following will need considering:

* Supply LT (SLT) is the time that follows from determining the need and deciding to place an order, up to the time it is available for issue. Accuracy of data is needed and the SLT includes many different steps, as shown by the earlier lead time explanation. SLT therefore includes the external suppliers' lead times, plus the internal steps of the requiring/ordering between customer/user and the receiving/available for issue lead times. It is surprising that many companies do not know objectively what their SLTs are. This simply means therefore they are not effectively controlling their inventory.

- Supply LT variability (SLTV) if applicable is also usually poorly dealt with; SLT must be measured on a continual basis to identify any variability.
- Average demand (AvD) or the forecasted demand during the supply lead time is sometimes called the lead time demand, which more correctly is the demand during the supply lead time.
- Demand variability (DV) if applicable is the difference between the average demand and the actual demand over time and it is measured by the standard deviation.
- Setting a required service level (S/L) ensures the correct stock level is held and is available to service requirements by covering against any supply and or demand uncertainty.

Where demand and supply lead times are certain, predictable and known then the calculations are easier; known and fixed supply lead times with known and fixed demand create for simpler decisions. For example:

Fixed demand   *50 units per week*

Supply LT   *2 weeks*

Then one order option is 100 units ordered every two weeks.

The keys to having such predictability are found for example where:

- historic demand and supply lead time are good proxies for the future;
- long mature product life cycles exist;
- no promotional product activity has been undertaken.

However, for most companies, such certainty is not the real world and conditions of uncertainty are normal. For example, the marketplace works against certainty with demand volatility and increased product variety by introducing new products and competition. Reduced and shorter product life cycles limit the value of historic data and, additionally, wider global supply bases cause complications for supply lead times.

All of these changes to demand and supply lead times mean greater safety stocks are required.

The following illustrates the calculations used to cover against the probability that we will be dealing with uncertainty:

Average demand (AvD)   *50 units per week*

Supply lead time (SLT)   *2 weeks*

Demand variability (DV)   *12 units*

Service level (S/L)   *95% (1.64 standard deviations)*

The overall formula is:

Reorder level (ROL) is equal to:

*AvD * SLT; for the cycle stock/demand lead time, plus*

*DV * S/L * √SLT; for the safety stock*

*Then 50 * 2*	=	*100 (cycle stock)*
*12 * 1.64 * √2*	=	*28 (safety stock)*
∴ ROL	=	*128*

To illustrate again the concept of variability, if we get SLT variability of 1 week (that is, SLT increases by 1 week):

*Then 50 * 3*	=	*150*	*(100 cycle stock)*
*12 * 1.64 * √3*	=	*34*	*(safety stock)*
∴ ROL	=	*184*	

Here the extra stock for the 1-week variability is:

50 (extra cycle stock) + 6 (extra safety stock) = 56

Some important conclusions are possible from this simple example:

- the longer the lead-time variability, the more safety stock is required;
- SLTV is critical.

Supply chain planning

The focus should always be towards customers, internal or external.

It should always be recalled that SCM is all about the horizontal flow of goods/materials, information and money. This movement will usually be across often vertical and bureaucratic functional silos. The horizontal flows and the vertical management silos will need to be integrated so that coordination of the flows are realised, for outcomes like growth, lower costs, improved service and so on.

From a strategic and tactical point of view, this will mean:

- restructuring internal organisational relationships;
- market evaluation;
- identifying different customer segments requiring individual supply/demand chains;
- developing synchronised relationships with suppliers and customers;

- implementing the enabling ICT.

MAIN AREAS IN SCM

The five main areas that affect the supply chain in any organisation will be as follows:

Supply chain(s) configuration

What and where are the decoupling points, for example the places where buying, making, moving and selling take place?

It is more than likely that the current configurations will be wrong, as different products and different customers require different supply chains. Also, the required performance levels will differ. Therefore, fundamental decisions are needed about what gets done, how it gets done and where it gets done for these different supply chains.

Management practices

What are the processes and practices that facilitate 'buy, make, move, and sell?'
When were these last examined and improved?
How open is the organisation to changing quickly? For example:

- joint planning and setting objectives with suppliers and customers on KPIs covering service, cycle times flexibility and stock levels;
- joint product development, strategic supplier relationships and vendor managed inventory;
- centralised stock holding, moving direct with single handling;
- in Europe, using assemble/pack to order planning and operations.

Relationships

How are suppliers and customers aligned?

- With suppliers – this can include close collaboration with extensive information sharing to total outsourcing.
- This can include becoming the preferred supplier/partner.

Building such relationships involves time, patience, commitment and ultimately trust. Companies will usually only do this, when they have a clear business strategy and clear core competencies. Courage and self-confidence then enables strategic relationships to be formed.

Organisation

How are cross-functional tasks and decisions carried out and undertaken?

Internal organisation and structure is critical. Accountability and authority for the entire supply chain is best wherever possible.

- If products are unique, then reporting into the appropriate business unit may be used.
- If portions of the supply chain are shared, then ownership may be in accordance with the functional organisation, for example localised or globalised.

Above all, what needs to happen is aligned performance objectives from end to end and aligned decision-making authority from end to end.

Information and communication technology

How is ICT used to support the integrated supply chain?

ICT is often the enabler for SCM improvement. It should not, however, be used in isolation from all the above.

STRATEGIC DESIGN

The points arising from these five main areas mean that supply chains need strategic design as follows:

Customer demand

- Design the supply chain on market needs, as it is demand that kick starts the whole process.
- Understand the supply chain requirement for customer segments and tailor as appropriate.

Product

- Products will vary; for example standard, segmented standard, customised standard, tailored customised, pure customised.
- Design products for interchange ability, ease of assembly and standardised parts.
- Assemble to order, customised products.
- Postpone final product differentiation until the product is required.

Strategy

- Management recognition, and commitment to the supply chain purpose/vision that recognises it is fundamental to integrate independent processes for interdependency, is needed.
- Concentrate on areas that have maximum business impact.
- Leverage e-business to link assets and process, across partners.
- Minimise fixed costs, keeping assets and resources flexible.
- As supply chains are collections of business that add value, then focus on the core value drivers. Then perform more added-value work.
- Outsource non-strategic and non-competitive activity (DIY or buy in).
- Adopt and enforce common performance and quality standards throughout the supply chain.

- Use flow logistics by designing all processes for the continuous flow of goods and information, therefore minimising lead times and stockholding.
- Design and manage adaptable supply chain networks.
- Manage through a cross-functional organisation and structure.
- Appreciate flexible relationships across the supply chain.
- Continually develop the people, so that they will continuously improve.
- Remember that supply chains may appear to be technically simple, but remain managerially difficult.

All the above decisions involve capital and risk, for example:

- Which products to sell?
- How many production plants?
- Which suppliers?
- What to stock and how much?
- What distribution network?
- Which of the above to make/buy in, or do self/outsource?

Supply chain key performance indicators

Supply chain performance will be driven by the following:

- organisational configuration of the physical assets and product/information flows (for example, elimination of inventory whilst optimally balancing costs, service levels and availability);
- management of the supply chain (for example, flexibility and reliance on quality);
- external relationships with suppliers and customers (for example, a share to gain approach);
- internal structures and management of the supply chain (for example, elimination of all barriers to all the internal and external activities);
- information systems (for example, transparent flows of goods/information).

FINANCIAL PERFORMANCE IN THE SUPPLY CHAIN

With SCM there can be some inherent problems with using traditional financial measures, for example with linking the financial outcome to:

- the input operational efficiencies, such as the utilisation of resources;
- the level of service delivered, such as the level of stock availability.

Additionally in financial terms, stock is viewed as an asset, as it is sold to realise money. However, SCM contributes and supplements the financial view, for example by:

- focusing on where assets are deployed and how these can be 'sweated' or used more productively; for example increasing volume throughput with fixed cost assets;
- turning over stock quicker, improving cash flow and reducing stock holding costs;

- freeing up capital invested in fixed asset by outsourcing, for example, reducing stock levels;
- integrating with external players to reduce exposure and foster concentration on core competencies.

When relating the Theory of Constraints (TOC) to the normal financial performance measures of companies (net profit, return on investment and cash flow), the view of TOC is very supportive by emphasising the importance of the supply chain operational aspects and the associated flows/throughputs with the inventory holdings and the costs.

Goldratt notes that the normal financial measures are all actually affected by the following operational measures:

- increases in throughput (in TOC, throughput is the rate at which money is generated by sales);
- reducing inventory (inventory is money invested, awaiting sale);
- reducing costs/operating expenses (money spent turning inventory into throughput).

Finally, the following aspects have been noted for obtaining profitable performance for a supply chain (based on 'How to survive in a volatile world', *Logistics Europe*, June 2002):

- Product and service portfolio management
  - Detect product life cycles shifts and modify underlying models.
  - Customer segmentation allows targeted service offerings that increase margins.
  - New products can capture the market potential more directly.
- Working capital efficiency
  - Reduce inventory and payment cycles.
  - Rapid flows without disruptive risk.
- Cost to serve
  - Cost management is reported by product and by channel.
  - Checking the planned to actual profitability of each customer order.
  - Use of TOC/TAC models.
- Asset efficiency
  - Utilisation of assets goes straight to the bottom line.
  - Outsourcing can reduce the amount of working capital needed as whoever owns the asset has the direct bottom line cost impact.
  - Tax efficiency from off balance sheet financing.
  - Contribute to maintain operational competitiveness whilst minimising global tax rate.

SUPPLY CHAIN PERFORMANCE DRIVERS

Supply chain performance will therefore be driven by all of the following aspects:

- organisational configuration of the physical assets and product/information flows (for example, elimination of inventory whilst optimally balancing costs, service levels and availability);
- management of the supply chain (for example, flexibility and a reliance on quality);

- external relationships with suppliers and customers (for example, a share to gain approach);
- internal structures and management of the supply chain (for example, elimination of all barriers to all the internal and external activities);
- information systems (for example, transparent flows of goods/information).

The entire supply chain performance can be measured by the following measurement tools:

Description	Measurement tool	Definition	Units
Customer orders fulfilment	On-time/in-full rate (OTIF)	Orders OTIF	%
	Lead time	Receipt of order to despatched/ delivered	Hours/days
Customer satisfaction	Customer survey	A sampling survey to ask for customers experiences, for example: – support available – product availability – flexibility – reliability – consistency – comparison to the competition	% satisfied
Supply management	OTIF	As above	%
	Supplier survey	As above customer survey	% satisfied
	Effectiveness	Year-over-year improvements	%
	Lead time	Time placed order to time available for use	Hours/days
Inventory (measure for each holding place of raw materials, work in progress and finished goods)	Forecast accuracy	Actual/forecast sales per SKU	%
	Availability	Ordered/delivered per SKU	%
	On hand	Value on hand/daily delivered value	Days
Cash flow	Cash to cash	Time from paying suppliers to time paid by customers	Days
Quality	Quality	Non conformances, as appropriate	Per 100 or 1000 or million
Operations	Utilisations	Used/available	Units
	Productivity	Actual/standard	Hours
	Costs	Actual/standard	Costs
	Lead times	Time start/time completed per operation, (see the earlier lead time section)	Hours/days

continued

People relationships	Internal	Absence rates	%
		Staff turnover rates	%
	Internal	Opinion surveys, for example: – support given – development – morale – work conditions – communication, etc.	% satisfied
	External	Sampling survey, as used in the above customer surveys	% satisfied
Costs	Total supply chain or per operation cost	Cost per time period/units	£ per unit

Supply chain metrics and strategies

No single strategy will ever sustain in the long run due to the ever-changing dynamic market and external demands. Supply chain strategies will need to be constantly worked on. Figure 1.13 shows one way to monitor the strategy.

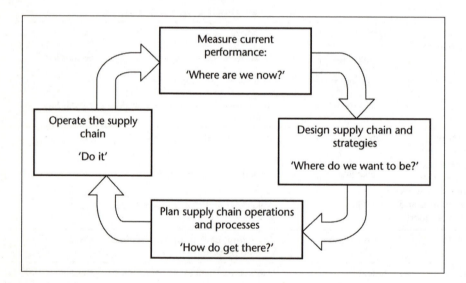

Figure 1.13   Monitoring the supply chain strategy

To assist in monitoring the supply chain further, the following questions may help:

- When were all of the lead times last examined?
- Have manufacturing and supply lead times been reduced in the last three years?
- When were all of the supply chain processes mapped?
- Were value-added and non-value added activities clearly identified?
- What barriers are there to increasing service and reducing costs?
- Are there multi-functional teams working on improving materials and information flow?
- Have lot sizes and set-up times been reduced in the last three years?

- Have all inventories been reduced in the last three years?
- Are inventory buffers in existence to protect against quality problems?
- Are there agreements with suppliers and mutually agreed goals for continuous improvement?
- Are suppliers certified to 'no inspection' required?
- Are communications fit for purpose and are electronic and face to face?
- Is lead time precisely known for replenishment and for customer deliveries?
- How much time is spent on expediting?
- Are performance measures weighted towards short lead times and quick response with minimal inventory levels?

Supportive supply chain management approaches

With SCM being dynamic and changing, then varied approaches and philosophies develop. Whilst some of these are new innovative approaches, other approaches often take one specific aspect of the supply chain (such as time compression), and then repackage it using a catchy new name (like 'quick response'). This is often then also reduced to a two- or three-letter abbreviation (like QR/ECR).

Such repackaging can of course be useful, as people will often better focus and identify with badges. These provide a clearer identification of the approach needed and therefore give direction.

We shall examine many of these approaches here, being specific about the total supply chain, distribution, inventory and financing.

It should be appreciated this division is arbitrary and there is overlap. For example, collaboration will be seen to be a common theme and this will therefore be looked at later in a separate section, where we shall also look specifically at other approaches like lean/agile, total quality management and reverse logistics.

MORE 'TOTAL SUPPLY CHAIN' APPROACHES

Quick response (QR)

QR was originally developed in the USA in the 1980s for the domestic apparel and textile industry. It was the 'badge' used to encourage national suppliers to react faster to compete with lower-priced international imports. It involves shorter lead times with reduced stock levels and demand lead times, so that a faster response can be made to customers order requirements. It requires adjusting the reorder levels and also closer working between suppliers/customers.

Efficient consumer response (ECR)

ECR is another USA abbreviation originally developed for fast-moving grocery products. It uses consumer demand to drive the supply chain to deliver exactly when required. Again it uses collaborative approaches supported by ICT.

Collaborative, planning, forecasting and replenishment (CPFR)

CPFR is a collection of business processes that are better enabled by a jointly agreed information system. It aims to change the relationship between suppliers and customers to create an accurate end-consumer-driven process and information flow. Suppliers and customers have a common view of consumer demand; they collaborate and coordinate plans, actions and activities through a jointly owned planning system to ensure product availability.

Using CPFR means that the organisation must:

- develop collaborative agreements (and we shall return soon to the subject of collaboration);
- create joint business plans;
- create sales forecasts;
- identify exceptions to the sales forecasts;
- resolve these exceptions;
- create the order forecast;
- identify exceptions to the order forecast;
- resolve these exceptions;
- generate the order.

It will be seen that collaboration is used to resolve the exceptions in forecasts. CPFR therefore looks to build business relationships by focusing on jointly managed processes with common communication tools. In summary, CPFR allows for planning rather than reacting, and uses ICT/Internet technology to reduce inventory and expense, while increasing sales and improving customer service. CPFR looks to improve the forward visibility of requirements across the entire supply chain.

MORE 'DISTRIBUTION' SUPPLY CHAIN SPECIFIC APPROACHES

Postponement

This represents coordinating and delaying the 'buy/make/move' activities so that they take place as close as possible to the 'sell' demand. Used especially for high-value goods that have a high demand uncertainty, postponement involves for example, assemble to order (ATO) at distribution centres (or with a partner downstream) that are located close to customers and can customise the order.

Consolidation

This is to benefit from economies in scale, especially of transport, for example:

- Retailers have primary consolidation centres (PCCs) located in regions near to suppliers where stock is held pending being 'called forward.' It is then consolidated with other suppliers' goods at the PCC into a full load delivered to each of the retailers, nationally located, regional distribution centres (RDCs). From the RDCs, products are either placed into stock or are immediately moved across the warehouse (cross-docked) on receipt for final delivery to the retailer's individual stores.

- Suppliers have national distribution centres (NDCs) that receive goods from factories/ production plants located in many different places, where the different products are mixed and then consolidated into loads for delivery to customers.
- Road transport companies have pallet networks which are used to combine goods from various suppliers into full loads for transhipment via a central hub onward to regional partners, who then undertake the final delivery.
- Forwarding companies offer 'groupage'/consolidation services between the UK to/from continental and global destinations.

INVENTORY-SPECIFIC APPROACHES

Vendor-managed inventory (VMI)

VMI involves suppliers holding stocks at customers' premises. It requires the sharing of information by customers, so that the supplier has visibility of the customers' demand and usage. The supplier is then able to control stock levels in customers' premises. Customer ownership takes place and the payment to the supplier is only made when the stock is used/sold.

For customers this clearly reduces costs and the risks of buying goods that will not be used or sold, and improves cash flow. For the supplier, VMI ties in the customer and they will have longer-term relationships. This however is at the expense of delayed payments and potential product returns. VMI can be especially useful when there is stable demand.

Co-managed inventory (CMI)

CMI involves joint working of suppliers with customers to satisfy demand by cooperatively managing inventory rather than handing the day-to-day management over totally to suppliers as happens in VMI. As it is a cooperative approach, information exchange (using appropriate systems such as EPOS, EDI, e-mail) combine with the development of better relationships, such as using cross-functional teams.

FINANCIALLY SPECIFIC APPROACHES

Direct product profitability (DPP)

This is an accounting technique to allocate fixed costs direct to specific products. It attempts to ensure that each SKU can be fully costed and compared to its selling price, so that profit can be specifically identified on a per-SKU basis.

DPP removes any overall average costing across all of the product range, as these will give distorted figures especially when the range of price and cost variability is high.

Essentially a tool used in retailing it is calculated as follows:

$$
\begin{aligned}
DPP \quad &= \quad \textit{Sales, less the cost of goods sold} \\
&= \quad \textit{Gross margin, plus allowances/discounts} \\
&= \quad \textit{Adjusted gross margin} \\
&\quad\;\; \textit{less warehouse costs} \\
&\quad\;\; \textit{less transport costs} \\
&\quad\;\; \textit{less retailing costs}
\end{aligned}
$$

Economic value added (EVA)

EVA, like DPP and activity-based costing, was developed to overcome weaknesses seen in traditional accounting practices. The concept is to deduct a charge for the amount of capital employed from the net operating profit. A positive EVA therefore means that value is being created, a negative one that value is being wasted and destroyed. EVA therefore assists in showing where the financial capital costs focus needs to be.

EVA however has its critics:

• Capital investment is reduced, so that the EVA ratio remains more positive.
• The use of capital is only one measure of a business and its use ignores the other measures that contribute to profit, such as innovation, market standing, people development, productivity and utilisation of other resources.
• Use of human capital and knowledge may actually be more critical than the financial capital of an organisation, for example in research, new product developments and designs.

QUALITY MANAGEMENT

Quality management has many parallels with SCM and is therefore very supportive in aims and ideals. Quality management represents the involvement and commitment of everyone in continually improving work processes to satisfy the requirements and expectations of all internal and external customers. It is therefore somewhat similar to SCM, as will be further seen in the ten basic principles of quality management:

• agreed customer requirements;
• understand and improve customer/supplier chains;
• do the right things;
• do things right first time;
• measure for success;
• continuous improvement is the goal;
• management must lead;
• training is essential;
• communicate more effectively;
• recognise successful involvement.

There are several options available to further these principles:

• *Kaizan* means continuous improvement in a gradual and ordered way. It has an objective of the elimination of waste in the processes, components and functions. Kaizan therefore has two parts: one being improvements and change, and the other being to do this ongoing and continually.

• *Total quality management* (TQM) is an approach towards larger-scale company change and improves existing process and functions. TQM needs strong direction and leading from the top as requires commitment and involvement from all. Middle management in traditional command and control structures can often be a barrier to TQM, as the managers fear a loss of control as their jobs become largely superfluous as involvement spreads below them.

- *Six Sigma* involves statistics, as in the use of the word 'sigma' meaning standard deviation. Statistics are used to establish company benchmarks that assist in work processes being continually improved to meet the customers' expectations. It has a goal that the chance of failure is only 3.4 in a million opportunities (this is six-sigma standard deviation). Whilst this may be unattainable, it does indicate that Six Sigma, like quality generally, often represents a 'journey to a destination'.

The six key concepts are:

- Critical quality: what actually is it that matters to the customer?
- Defects: what happens when we fail to deliver what the customer wants?
- Process capability: what can the processes do?
- Variation: what is the customer's perception and how does this differ from the critical quality?
- Stable operations: what has to be done to ensure consistent and certain processes?
- Design for six sigma: what is involved in designing to meet customer needs and to get process capability?

REVERSE LOGISTICS

This may be defined as 'the management of returns from users back to senders', 'the management of returns from stores back to: the store for resale, to the supplier, to consumers through appropriate channels or for disposal' or as 'closing the supply-chain loop by recapturing the value'.

The process involved is collection – return to designated site – check condition – collate – recover/disposal – redistribution. The keys areas are as follows:

- the technology/information to say why they are to be returned: are they faulty, are they damaged, are they not needed (for example, clothing catalogue goods returns = 18–35 per cent, electrical catalogue returns = 4–5 per cent);
- the sender's scanning and tagging, if any;
- the process of coming back (for example, collection by delivery vehicles, assessment, categorising);
- the feedback and performance information (for example, to buyers/marketing). Life cycle product costing approaches from cradle to grave are emphasised here;
- the assessment on receipt and the disposal options (see below), and the space required to do this (do offsite?);
- the returns policy of the companies involved (for example, the supplier's and the retailer's policies may vary);
- the full financial implications of the process.

Inspection is needed by expert eyes in recovery and disposal, the basic options being:

- no change to the original state, that is re-use of overstocks, excess inventory;
- dismantle to re-use, that is recover/remanufacture or refurbish;

- extracting of elements to be used as raw material elsewhere, that is repair/reconditioning of damaged products, replace missing components, recover of packaging and product;
- return to supplier perhaps for disassembly into parts for recycling;
- disposal.

These options then may involve restock, resale or scrap of obsolete products/parts. Finally there will be a need to consider all the legal implications and environmental restrictions.

2 *People Relationships at Work*

> *In order for people to be happy in their work, three things are needed: they must be fit for it; they must not do too much of it; and they must have a sense of success in it.*

John Ruskin in *Pre-Raphaelitism* (1851)

> *If you look at what goes wrong ... more than half of the problems are people issues.*

Andrew Wolstenholme, Construction Director, London Heathrow Terminal Five

> *Running a business is not always a matter of logic and mathematics. It is just as much a question of understanding the psychological impact.*

Jan Carlzon in *Moments of Truth* (1987)

In this part we explore that, whilst supply chain management may be technically simple, it remains managerially difficult. People relationships are therefore important. We examine the behavioural patterns and styles found at work and in business. We establish that people use different management styles and look at models of leadership and vision in management.

People work both as individuals and also together in teams. They combine through task completion and job responsibility into a specific company culture.

Team relationships are next explored along with team building and the ongoing skills needed. Case studies are used to show important principles.

We next look at company cultures and examine formal and informal cultures and how these interact with purpose, power and people relationships. In order to get the best from people, the key is motivation and this is examined with best practice. We conclude by looking at empowerment, and compare and contrast this with traditional command and control methods.

Our approach in this part of the book is to highlight briefly those key people relationship areas that have to be impacted to ensure that SCM will work for business benefit.

People relationships are important

It is our view that people relationships are important and are ignored at the peril of inviting subsequent problems. In the early 1990s Stuart Emmett was working with a colleague to develop a training programme on SCM. At the time, this was a pioneering programme and whilst this covered all the (subsequently) well-known topics, like demand, inventory, purchasing, production, transport, warehousing, IT and so on, we also wanted to include something on relationships and people management to show that SCM needed to be integrated and coordinated 'in the minds of people' as well as through 'technical tools, systems and techniques'.

Stuart's more technically minded colleague however could not see this and insisted that the course could not cover what he saw as 'people crap'.

We did eventually cover 'people', but chose not to use the rest of the description.

This story does illustrate that some people will have difficulty in seeing that people and management are connected. However, as Peter Drucker has noted:

> *Because the object of management is a human community held together by the work bond for a common purpose, management always deals with the nature of Man.*

We do therefore cover some aspects of people's nature and how it relates to people management. Whilst there are thousands of texts that cover this subject, our approach will be to highlight briefly those key relationships areas that have to be impacted to ensure that SCM will work for business benefit.

As a further support for this emphasis on this topic, please consider the following 'three guiding principles for the future' (Source: The Work Foundation (formerly The Industrial Society), in their 2003 *Working Capital* report):

1. *From hierarchy to networks:*
   Leadership styles must change.
   Command and control hierarchies are no longer working.

2. *From tangible to intangible assets:*
   Competitive advantage now comes from knowledge, relationships, values and networks.

3. *From paternalism to consumerism:*
   The rhetoric on customer service has moved on from supply led to being demand led.

Principle 1 clearly makes a statement on 'people' style and on structures. Principle 2 is clear on where competitive advantage comes from and includes knowledge/relationships/values (which are 'within' people), and from networks (also known as the supply chain). Principle 3 has been well documented in Part 1 of this book.

Therefore all of these three principles from The Work Foundation have clear implications for what is done in the supply chain.

RELATIONSHIPS ARE FUNDAMENTAL TO SUPPLY CHAIN MANAGEMENT

SCM has, as a key principle, individual businesses coming together to integrate, coordinate and control their supplier/customer activities of buying, making, moving and selling.

Whilst SCM may be technically simple, it is usually managerially difficult; it is how the relationships are handled, with all internal and external supply chain players, that will be fundamental to the efficiency and the effectiveness of the overall supply chains involved.

Improving the people relationships is therefore one of the main keys for better SCM. Do you for example know of any relationship (business or otherwise) that cannot be improved? In our experience, most of them can be.

Furthermore, the view that a company is able to do something by itself is a dangerous myth that obscures the reality that a company only ever does anything as a result of its people doing something. Too many people, usually unconsciously, ignore the plain fact that it is the people who are the key element in all companies. We can only ever get to the core of any business through and by dealing with people relationships.

The financial lead view and 'hard side' of business becomes an increasing difficult one to predict in fast-changing global economies. Looking at what has happened when company performance fails dramatically through receivership shows the importance of people relationships. Receivers have identified the following three causes of failure:

- lack of information, meaning, for example, a limited view of options;
- lack of top-team balance, meaning, for example, there is little challenge with negative compliance as boards are too similar and do not have the required depth or breadth;
- lack of others' opinions, for example an autocratic CEO who goes only for say, growth – one-man rule with non-participating boards is found.

It seems here that wider views and lack of open debate amongst people were missing. Autocratic management seems to have prevented any positive conflict of ideas. Company performance and profitability have failed and can be directly linked to the lack of open debate and consideration of wider viewpoints. If relationships had been improved, then the companies may have survived.

Understanding individuals

People are therefore the foundation of business relationships. Therefore to understand how these relationships work, we need to have some understanding of individuals. Figure 2.1 gives a view of people behaviour.

It is beliefs that ultimately drive what we say or do and this is visible as our unique style of our behaviour. Beliefs are what is true for that person and represent the substance of a person. In turn, beliefs create values that influence the attitudes and preconditions that are held and direct how we think, feel about things and make choices.

Habits are then the visible repeated and learned behaviour patterns, and to change a habit, there is a need to change the attitude that created it. For a deep-rooted habit to change, then the invisible values and beliefs will also have to be changed.

A difficulty here, however, is about perception or how we see things; after all perception is reality (at least it is always so for us, if not for others).

Remember the following about perception:

- Perception is 90 per cent behind the eyes.
- Whether you see it wrong or see it right, you are right.
- As a person thinks, so they are.
- Do you see the glass of water as half full, or half empty?

Where perceptions are shared then we have agreement; where they are not, disagreement.

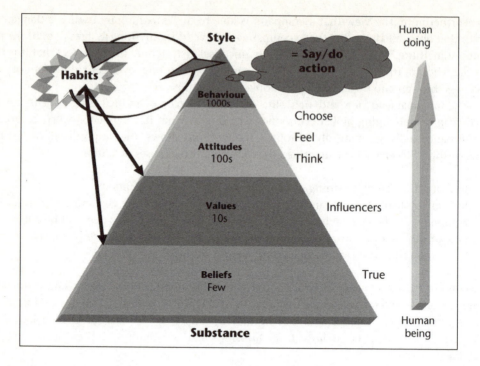

Figure 2.1   Behaviour

Changing perceptions though is not always going to be easy and whilst in both philosophy and action it can look simple, the reality for most people is that we all have both culture and gender influencers that mould us into particular reactions and types of behaviour. For example:
Men are encouraged from birth to:

- be tough;
- be strong;
- be in control;
- not back down;
- give as good as you get;
- show no weakness;
- win if you can, never mind the cost.

Women are encouraged from birth to:

- be gentle;
- to follow;
- be compassionate;
- put others before themselves;
- to share;
- not to argue;
- not to get angry.

This also gets us into the classic 'nature or nurture' debate: are we born and stay as we are born, or are we a blank canvas at birth that is made by our environment and surrounding influences? Whichever is dominant will influence our life.

PEOPLE DIFFER

As adults, business cultures and management cultures will have an impact of how people behave at work; for example, consider the difference between local government and Tesco.

People differ and therefore respond differently. For example, some people see problems as adversity and pain. Conversely, with other people problems are opportunities and are seen as potential victories and gains. One has learnt to be helpless; the other has learnt to live.

Another view of different responses/styles follows and compares different types of people climbing a mountain; perhaps a good analogy for doing something hard and different from the norm?

Quitters	Campers	Climbers
Abandons early	Goes half way	Gets there
'Too hard'	'Comfortable here'	'Not there yet, let's go'
Survives	Vegetates	Grows
Do just enough	Analyses	Takes risks
Defends	Some progress is made	'Energiser bunny'
Blames others	Gets too tired	Achieves
Rejects change	Waits and sees what will happen	Accepts change
Can be disruptive	Can be subversive	Embraces change
Says in the rut	WIIFM (what's in it for me)	Looks for the next peak
20% of people?	60% of people?	20% of people?

It is perhaps no surprise therefore that relationships in companies and between companies will differ greatly. Whereas a few companies would seem to recognise this, what remains a surprise however is that there does not seem to be a wider recognition of this. It seems that each person's/company's perception remains their reality to the exclusion of recognising differences and the exclusion of exploring doing things differently. Much learning and changing seems to be needed.

Individual management styles

Given their different behaviour it follows from the mix of individualism, collective groups/teams and a company culture, coupled with national cultures, that individuals at work will display different management styles.

Such styles may be normal and natural and used unconsciously. Alternatively a specific style may be selected consciously and deliberately for use at the right time and the right place in the right circumstances.

An 'extremes' view follows to give a broad, polarised view of management styles.

An autocratic and aggressive manager:

- drives and pushes people but is not a leader;
- has a single viewpoint;
- is a one-way communicator;
- is demanding – 'do it my way, now';
- takes fixed my-way positions with a contest of will;
- makes threats and applies pressure.

A procrastinator and passive manager:

- abdicates from taking decisions;
- uses group viewpoints;
- is indecisive and believes they are always democratic;
- 'what do you all want to do, whenever';
- changes positions easily and avoids any contest;
- makes offers and yields to pressure.

A charismatic and assertive manager:

- pulls more than pushes;
- is a two-way communicator;
- is followed naturally as a leader;
- makes concessions – 'I think this, what do we think';
- solves problems and explores interests;
- views partnerships and reasons;
- looks for objective criteria and yields to principles not pressure.

Positional and partnership models of negotiations

Another view of different individual styles is found in the following model of negotiation style:

Hard positioning bargaining	Partnership negotiation	Soft positioning bargaining
Adversary participation	Problem-solving participants	Friendly participants
Goal is victory	Wise outcome is reached, amicably and efficiently	Goal is agreement
Demand concessions	Separate the people from the problem	Make concessions
Hard on people and the problem	Be soft on the people but hard on the problem	Soft on people and the problem
Distrust	Mutual trust	Trust others blindly
Dig in and maintain position	Focus on interests not positions	Change position easily
Make threats	Explore interests	Make offers
Mislead what the bottom line is	Avoid having a bottom line	Disclose the bottom line

Hard positioning bargaining	Partnership negotiation	Soft positioning bargaining
Demand one-sided gains	Invent options for mutual gain	Accept one-sided losses to reach agreement
Insist on your position	Develop mutual options and decide later	Insist on agreement
Try to win a contest of will	Insist on objective criteria	Tries to avoid a contest of will
Apply pressure	Reason and be open to reasons, yield to principle not pressure	Yield to pressure

Another view on styles is the following old and the new ways – another 'extremes' view. Managing with a command and control style:

- keeps control;
- 'holds onto' people;
- is judgemental;
- 'tells';
- sees though a 'pinhole';
- is directive;
- takes a 'push' approach.

Managing with a coaching or empowering style:

- lets people try;
- gives people 'self-release';
- is non-judgmental;
- 'sells';
- sees the wider view;
- is supportive;
- takes a 'pull' approach.

Managers may also be leaders but there are many views of what this means; the following represents another 'extremes' view.

Manager	Leader
Handles tactics, drives forward using authority	Handles strategy, drives forward by using inspiration and goodwill
Makes the provision and the 'how'	Makes the vision and the 'why'
Work is managed to a satisfactory performance	People are led and influenced beyond simple legitimate authority
Plans the pace and reacts	Directs and is proactive
'Fire-fights'	'Fire-lights'
Works with boundaries/ limits and demands respect	Works with hopes and dreams and commands respect
Mainly is short term	Mainly is medium/longer term
Inspires stability within the 'status quo'	Inspires innovation and change
Often are extraverts and emotionally warm	Often are introverts and emotionally distant

Some comments on the subject have also been noted as follows:

- Leaders choose the things to do and managers then do them right.
- You can be a terrific manager but a poor leader.
- A leader can get people to do something they do not even know why they are doing it; they just do it.
- Leadership and management is definitely different.

MODEL OF LEADERSHIP

The following represents the view taken in this book. Whether transactional leadership is more what a manager does and transformational leadership is more what a leader does is not really the issue, as companies need both.

Feature	Transactional	Transformational
Vision	Goals and objectives for immediate results	Long-term vision
Control	Structures and processes created; solves problems	Creates climate of trust and empowers people to control themselves; manages problem solving
Outlook	Maintain and improve the current situation	Changes the current situation
Style	Plan, organises, directs and controls people	Coaches and develops people
Culture	Guards and defends	Challenges and changes
Power	From position and authority within the organisation	From influencing a network of relationships

VISION IN MANAGEMENT

To move forward and make changes in direction, having a vision is useful. We will look later at SCM visioning; meanwhile, a vision is something that describes:

- where you want to be;
- what you want to create;
- what you can commit to;
- what you believe in.

It is:

- more timeless and enduring (than yearly determined goals and objectives);
- collective aspirations;
- a shared commitment;
- the 'passion of vision' (as it needs to be deeply held).

Vision involves having hindsight and foresight as follows:

- Review and recognise what has gone well, what has gone wrong.
- Acknowledge what could have been better.
- Think of achievement(s) wanted.
- Wind the clock forward.
- Picture things in 12 months.
- What does the picture look like?
- Doing well?
- Everyone working together?
- Are they inspired?
- Do they take responsibility?
- Everyone looking for ways to improve?
- What are the energy levels?
- What do want to see different?
- What do want to hear others saying about their colleagues, their department, the company?
- What do you feel about your role, your people and your organisation in 12 months?

The challenge to management from visioning is therefore:

- Is the image created different from the 'now'?
- What needs to be done to get others to see the view they see?
- What three things are needed to be done now to start to change things?

Getting the best for people is not always going to be an easy or an automatic process for leaders or for managers. As noted already, people operate on at least three levels: firstly as individuals in their own right, secondly in collective groups and teams who will then, thirdly, combine into a company/culture.

Team relationships

Teams involve a small number of people who have a common shared and accepted goal. The goal is the 'performance purpose' and the team players, the people, have a complementary contribution with mutual accountability. Commitment to teams involves putting the team before individuals; however, teams require the right blend of unique individual strengths.

The following can be said about teams:

- Individual success is dependent on others.
- Teams work out problems together, individual blame is banished.
- The whole is more than the sum of the parts.
- Teams require individuals to connect to something bigger than them.
- You need to be awake, aware and in tune with others.
- United we stand but divided we fall.
- There is none of us as strong as all of us.

In the supply chain, cross-functional teams can be very helpful and fundamental to the integration of both the internal supply chain and also of the internal/external supply chains of organisations. We will return to this later.

Meanwhile the problem symptoms in teams can be readily noticed:

- Is there a high level of moaning and complaining?
- Is there a lack of respect for the team leader?
- Are there people in the team who refuse to speak to each other?
- Is vital collaboration being avoided?
- Are the team meetings brief and infrequent?
- Is it rare for people to say what they really feel about each other?
- Is the quality of work suffering?
- Is there a high level of sickness absence?

Sports teams offer some good analogies for work teams and the following aspects identified from the British Lions Rugby team of 1997 can be checked and compared with teams in organisations:

- inspired leadership;
- clear goal;
- meticulous planning;
- picking the right players;
- clear communication;
- excellent team spirit;
- committed team member;
- a learning culture;
- desire and passion;
- focus on results;
- shared values;
- self and team belief;
- confidence in ability;
- pride;
- celebrate success.

A key principle that is also demonstrated here is that teams require the right blending of unique individual strengths.

DIVERSITY

When managing people, it is important to be able to build and develop on strengths, and to recognise and manage weaknesses. Recognising diversity can therefore be seen as a strength, as some people are better at planning, some are better in organising process and methods, some are better able to meet deadlines, some at being directive, creative or thoughtful, are better at being supportive or at being utility players and flexible. After all, if all people were exactly the same, then we would all go fast in one direction and cause casualties en route.

Effective teams are therefore those that have selected the right mix of people and have determined the team values, vision and objectives. An example of a team value statement follows:

We, as a team, are committed to the following at place x on date y:

- *We will use the right language in all our external dealings with others.*
- *We will be open with each other in the team.*
- *We will support each other, especially in front of others.*
- *We will have the confidence to confront each other.*
- *We will deliver quality work.*

Effective teams will communicate and understand each other whilst motivating and supporting each other. The behaviours needed involve a blended mix of 'togetherness' and 'self'. Involvement and commitment require openness and, sometimes, confrontation with honesty and truthfulness in a supporting and trusting way.

TEAM-BUILDING STAGES

Putting together a collection of individuals does not make a team. It can require hard work until that right mix and blend is found. In building teams then the following stages and emotions are involved:

Stage 1 – Forming:

- excitement, anticipation and optimism;
- pride in being selected for the project;
- initial, tentative attachment to the team;
- suspicion, fear and or anxiety about the job ahead.

These behaviours can be observed:

- attempts to define the task and decide how it will be accomplished;
- attempts to determine acceptable group behaviour and how to deal with group problems;
- decisions on what information needs to be gathered;
- discussions of symptoms or problems not relevant to the task;
- difficulty in identifying relevant problems;
- complaints about the organisation and barriers to the task.

Stage 2 – Storming:

- resistance to the task and to quality improvement approaches different from what each individual member is comfortable using;
- sharp fluctuations in attitude about the team and the projects chance of success.

These behaviours can be observed:

- arguing among members even when they agree on the real issue;
- defensiveness and competition, factions choosing sides;

- questioning the wisdom of those who selected this project and appointed the other members of the team;
- establishing unrealistic goals, concern about excessive work;
- a perceived pecking order, disunity, increased tension and perhaps jealousy.

Stage 3 – Norming:

- a new ability to express criticism constructively;
- acceptance of membership in the team;
- relief that it seems everything is going to work out.

These behaviours can be observed:

- an attempt to achieve harmony by avoiding conflict;
- more friendliness, confiding in each other and sharing of personal problems;
- discussing the team's dynamics;
- a sense of team cohesion, a common spirit and goals;
- establishing and maintaining team ground rules and boundaries.

Stage 4 – Performing:

- members having insights into personal and group processes and better understanding of each others' strengths and weakness (remember that a weakness can often be a strength overdone);
- satisfaction at the team's progress.

These behaviours can be observed:

- constructive self-change;
- ability to prevent or work through group problems;
- close attachment to the team.

Stage 5 – Mourning or ending:

- sense of loss and sadness;
- wondering what happens next.

These behaviours can be observed:

- high and low emotions;
- leaving the past and going forward or;
- staying locked into the past.

There is much in these stages about how people respond and relate to each other. Our feelings come out of attitudes, beliefs and values and our behaviour is what is visible from our actions. A team coming together will pass through the above stages. However, before becoming an effective team it may get delayed or, at worst, stuck in the storming stage.

What is also important to realise here is that each stage up to Performing is a part of the process of forming effective teamworking and each stage will only move forward when each previous stage has been accepted and dealt with. It will also be seen how feelings and behaviour needs to change before reaching the performing stage.

Hopefully the performing stage continues for some time, but it can change even if one key member of the team leaves. When a team disbands or falls apart there is the stage of mourning and this is another change process that also needs to be managed.

The team-building stages are a good proxy for relationships. The following chart shows how the various team-building stages are related to Maslow's view of motivation and to business growth stages:

Relationships between motivation, business growth and teams

Level number and descriptor	Maslow on motivation	Business growth stages	Team building stages
5 Mastery	Self-actualise	Cost and/or service leader	Performing/ commitment
4 Understanding	Self-esteem	Control/revenue and service enhancement	Performing/ commitment
3 Awareness	Social	Growth/revenue and service	Norming/trials
2 Developmental	Safety	Sustain and maintain/ cost minimisation	Storming/learning
1 Start/foundational	Secure	Survival/cost reduction	Forming

It requires continual effort to move from level to level. It also requires effort to maintain each level. The above also shows that this is unlikely to happen by chance.

EFFECTIVE TEAMS

To have effective teamworking, then action that is needed which includes the following:

- selecting the right mix of people;
- determining the team vision and objectives;
- communicating and understanding each other;
- motivating and supporting each other;
- rewarding and rejoicing in good performance;
- reviewing team performance regularly.

The following behaviours will be needed:

- a blended 'mix' and 'give up self';
- involvement and commitment;
- openness and confrontation;
- honesty and truthfulness;
- support and trust;

- development and mediation;
- socialising.

TEAMWORKING SKILLS

Teamwork requires continual skills from all its members, including the following:

- listening;
- supporting;
- trusting;
- valuing others' contributions and ideas;
- giving the benefit of any doubt;
- recognising uniqueness;
- accepting fully the team view;
- openness and challenge/confrontation;
- centred leadership.

CHECKLIST: OVERALL TEAM REVIEW AND MONITOR

Objective:

- Do the team clearly understand and accept it?
- Are the goals clear and agreed?

Standards:

- Do they know what standards of performance are expected?

Size:

- Is the size correct (3 or 4 minimum, 6 to 8 is the optimum to allow for the right blend and mix of talent and skills)?

Team members and roles:

- Are the right individuals together?
- Are sub-groups needed?
- Are roles clear and accepted?

Team spirit:

- Are there opportunities for teamwork in jobs?
- Do pay and bonus help or hinder team spirit?
- Are interpersonal relationships positive?

Discipline:

- Are rules reasonable?
- Are they fair and impartially enforced?

Grievances:

- Are they dealt with promptly?
- Are matters that may disrupt the group dealt with?

Consultation:

- Is it genuine?
- Are ideas and suggestions encouraged?

Briefing:

- Is it regular?
- Does it cover current and future progress?

Support:

- Do I represent and support the team when talking to individuals when the team is apart?

Building people relationships

We start here with a look at individuals, management styles and team relationships and this moves us into building people relationships.

VIEWPOINT

FISHER AND BROWN, *GETTING TOGETHER*; THREE COMMON BELIEFS WHICH ARE POOR CHOICES IN BUILDING RELATIONSHIPS

1. Avoiding disagreement is good for the relationship.
   'To avoid disagreement, I should either give in or sweep a problem under the carpet.'

2. There is a trade-off between substantive interests and a good relationship.
   'I can risk the relationship to get what I want, or I can sacrifice my interests for the sake of the relationship, but I can't have both.'

3. Reciprocity is a good guideline for how to treat others.
   'To improve the relationship, I should either take the first step and hope that they reciprocate, or I should wait for them to go first and then respond, depending upon what they do.'

Fisher and Brown then go on to state, 'The goal for all relationships is to establish and maintain

---

those qualities that make it a good working relationship – one that is able to deal well with differences.'
This depends on the following basic elements:

- balance, reason and emotion;
- understanding;
- good communication skills;
- reliability;
- persuasiveness – it is more helpful than coercion;
- being accepting.

Now let us look at some more positive approaches. The following model examines the advantages and benefits of a more collaborative approach:

Unconditionally constructive advice	Good for the relationship because:	Good for me because:
Balance emotion with reason	An irrational battle is less likely	I make fewer mistakes
Try to understand	The better I understand you, the fewer collisions we will have	The less I shoot in the dark, the better solutions I can invent and the better able I am to influence you
Inquire, consult and listen	We both participate in making decisions; better communication improves them	I reduce the risk of making a mistake without giving up the ability to decide
Be reliable	It tends to build trust and confidence	My words will have more impact
Be open to persuasion; try to persuade	If people are persuaded rather than coerced, both the outcome and compliance are better	By being open, I keep learning; it is easier to resist coercion if one is open to persuasion
Accept the other as worth dealing with and learning from	To deal well with our differences, I have to deal with you and have an open mind	By dealing with you and reality, I can remove obstacles to learning the facts and to persuading you on the merits

Work/company culture

People working for a specific company find that it has its own way of doing things. For example, those people who leave one company to join another company to do a similar job will appreciate the urgent and early need to fit in. A company therefore has its own culture, which can be defined as 'the way we do things around here'. This will be shown both formally and informally.

FORMAL CULTURE

Company culture can therefore be shown by the overt and published vision, mission and goals and in the rules, norms and procedures of a company, for example:

- Vision incorporates the timeless values and beliefs.
- Mission incorporates the purpose, policies and power structures to achieve the task.
- Goals are the strategic, tactical and operational objectives, right down to people's individual roles and responsibilities.

All of these are important for the efficient running of the company and also to give overall direction, guidance and checkpoints.

Rules are needed to set standards of conduct and show the way people should behave by clarifying what is expected. Rules need to be:

- kept simple, clear and easy to understand;
- in writing;
- displayed publicly;
- kept up to date.

Procedures are also needed to help people keep to the rules and establish the methods used to deal with the rules. Procedures maintain and apply the standards, demonstrate a fair and consistent approach and also bring clarity. Such rules and procedures, therefore, represent an overt demonstration of the company culture.

INFORMAL CULTURE

However, culture is also often covert and informal, with values and beliefs that can remain unspecified. For example, contrast the difference between a charity and a private sector company, between the army and a football team, between the civil service and a retailer, between the Royal Mail and TNT. As well as things like dress, office styles and types of buildings, differences will be found in the human 'software' represented by the attitudes, values and beliefs that operate behind the scenes and which operate and determine how decisions are made.

TOTAL CULTURE

In all forms of management therefore, there are hard, objective and clearly defined ways of managing and there are also, the more subjective beliefs, values and soft skills involved. Culture therefore will embody the following:

- Purpose, policies and roles:
  - What are the structures/processes?
  - Where are the key decision makers?

This is the 'why?' and the 'what?' of the company.

- Power:
  - Who has access to which resources?

—   Where is the central authority?

This is the 'where and when of decision making?' of the company.

- People partnerships:
  —   What is the degree of support and trust?
  —   What is valued and what are the associated reward structures?

This is the 'with whom?' and the 'how?' of the company.

It may be that purpose and power are in fact easier to change than the people beliefs, attitudes and behaviour of the individuals that make up one part of the company culture. The following test can therefore be undertaken by talking to or observing, the people in a company. This will give indications on what the people aspects actually are:

Friendly	Unfriendly
People take the initiative	People feel boxed in
Teamwork flourishes	There is friction and a lack of appreciation between team members
People understand their contribution	People have little understanding of their role
Clear direction is found	Conflicting goals are found
Good communication exists	Mixed messages and little understanding exist
An even workload allowing for individual skills/ abilities	Work is spread unevenly
Teams know other team members' skills/abilities	Little understanding exists of what makes the team tick
Work environment is conducive to good performance	Physical environment prevents good performance

This quick test will show the management tasks that may be needed to improve work, for example:

- communicating regularly; for example, what do people think about their work and what do they want to do?
- creating a shared vision; for example, so that everyone knows where they are going;
- improving the physical environment; for example, lighting;
- using ideas from the team to make improvements to the work;
- using people playing to their strengths; for example, considering people's skills and aspirations and allocating work accordingly.

Management will ultimately involve getting the best performance possible and will therefore require:

- improving individual, team and company performance;
- motivating, developing and releasing people potential;
- designing, reflecting and supporting the company culture, strategy and style;

- communicating to people what is expected, what they are rewarded for, how they should deliver results and what results the company wants;
- consistency in leadership, the way people are treated, the way people operate and in the culture, purpose and strategy of the business.

This will also mean that the following is unhelpful:

- unclear direction(s);
- weak values;
- vague and inequitable objectives;
- variable appraisals/reviews;
- poor performance and motivation;
- inadequate training and development;
- bureaucracy;
- poor communications.

A prerequisite, therefore, for organisations, teams and individuals is to have:

- a clear picture of where the company/section/department is going;
- communication by management of the purpose, strategy, values and standards of behaviour expected.

For managers this means they should:

- develop an awareness of their impact on others;
- try always to involve people;
- believe that teamwork is the best approach;
- have a consistent management style;
- spend time coaching and developing;
- build a positive climate and motivate individuals and the team;
- empower team members rather than control them;
- develop appropriate performance reviews systems and methods;
- set challenging achievable and measurable objectives;
- communicate;
- reward success;
- agree improvements;
- give regular feedback.

MOTIVATION AT WORK

To provide motivation at work, according to theories on motivation (especially Herzburg), regard should be given to incentives and disincentives.

Incentives should be promoted, the sources for motivations being:

- achievements; for example, targets, smart objectives, interesting work;
- recognition; for example, creating heroes, appreciation;
- participation/responsibility; for example, involvement, consensus management;

- growth/prospects; for example, personal development, lifelong learning;
- feedback/communication; for example, praising and criticising fairly.

Key aspects with incentives are that, once provided, motivators do not last, as once we get our needs satisfied, the incentive reduces its impact. So for example, money by itself is not a motivator. It is important therefore to always have the 'motivation encore' ready to go beyond the temporary effect of a single motivator.

Disincentives should be cleaned up and eliminated, the sources of discontent to be removed being:

- policy/administration; for example, excessive paperwork, rules and procedures;
- supervision; for example, poor management styles, communication;
- working conditions; for example, inadequate heat, light, tidiness, safety equipment;
- personal relationships; for example, harassment, social facilities, shift patterns;
- salary/pay/ benefits; for example, comparison with others, times of reviewing;
- job security; for example, communication, job descriptions.

A key point with disincentives is that removing discontent does not bring motivation as it merely removes the discontent and stops that particular source of 'groan and moans'. If the discontent is not removed, it can create resentment, grow into a problem, cause grievance and lead onto dissatisfaction, depression, frustration, poor work and the use of disciplinary procedures.

Disincentives are also the root of work-related stress, or more correctly 'distress'.

IMPLEMENTING MOTIVATION

As mentioned above, motivation does not last: there is the need to look for the encore and you could run out of them. For example, where motivation is by fear ('do or else') or motivation is by reward ('do this and you get a prize'), once the fear or reward has gone, then so has the motivation.

The only motivation that will ever last is one that satisfies an individual's core values/ beliefs; for example, a belief that they will live life to the full gives an internal drive, which has an irresistible momentum. This links to the way that people believe and is also shown by the following statements:

- You are what you think.
- You get what you expect.
- The impossible is what no-one can do, until someone does.
- See yourself as a winner.
- Dream big dreams.
- Choose to be what you love.

Consequently when dealing with people, it is helpful to really know them and understand what needs are important to them. It helps to appreciate that the differences in people can be interesting, and that some people need more direction and guidance than others. Seeing things from another person's perspective will also help. This involves a manager or supervisor being able to:

- link motivation to specific staff;
- plan and organise what to do;

- develop positive habits themselves;
- plan motivating action points, by calendar events (for example, Christmas), by company events (for example, new recruits), by communication events (for example, newsletters), by personal events (for example, five-year service awards);
- keep a record on motivation actions for specific staff;
- review and check what happens and modify as appropriate.
  Effective motivation does really make a difference and it has been said:
- There are more chrysalises than butterflies – a manager's job is to encourage the chrysalis to hatch and to encourage the butterfly to fly.
- It is like getting a plant to bloom.

Motivation is not therefore, just about what you do to someone; it is more about what you allow them to do to themselves. This is also what empowerment is about, as we shall see shortly. However, there is always much that can be encouraged and supported by managers in the workplace and the following motivation model will help to ensure this is done.

Motivation model

Step 1 – Expect the best from your people

- Believe people want to do a good job.
- Tell people what is expected.
- Have clear rules and procedures (but do not be bureaucratic).
- Set SMART objectives/targets (SMART meaning those that are simple, measurable, attainable/achievable, realistic, timely).
- Involve people in determining these.
- Communicate.
- Be flexible, recognising that people are different.

Step 2 – Eliminate barriers to 'being the best'

- Check out all the disincentives and remove/improve as appropriate.
- Check out all the incentives and apply as appropriate.
- Make work interesting, meaningful and valuable.
- Ensure people have the appropriate resources to do the job as required.

Step 3 – Encourage people to 'be the best'

- Recognise good work.
- Give feedback.
- Be accessible, ask and listen for feedback.
- Reward with good pay, promotions and personal loyalty.

CASE STUDY
ELECTRICAL RETAILER'S MOTIVATION

Survey results
- 94 per cent of staff love working there.
- Absence is less than 2 per cent (national average is 4–5 per cent).

Management challenge is seen as:
- to make work fun;
- if people enjoy work ,then they do it better;
- be serious about staff satisfaction.

All directors spend 2 months per year on the shop floor.

Staff rewards include:
- free holidays;
- suggestion scheme: each one gets £25, every three months the best two get more money, give many small prizes, use good ideas and give back a proportion of the benefit;
- training, minimum twice a year top-up.

EMPOWERMENT

This is a concept that is related to motivation, the word meaning literally to give power. It involves looking at the management areas of responsibility, training, trust and support and it leads more towards a coaching style of management.

In normal management, the manager is accountable and responsible, but individual subordinates are responsible. In collective teams, however, both accountability and responsibility are shared and agreed. Accountability is represented by the view of a referee, who has the ultimate control that cannot be delegated or passed on by the team. Responsibility comes from all the players, who carry out simply what has to be done; for example, the duty of care in law and in health and safety.

Empowerment gives people a sense of ownership so they can see how what they do will fit in the bigger picture. Empowered people should therefore be able to:

- evaluate others' work;
- plan and schedule work;
- recruit and select;
- give presentations;
- determine the pace of work;
- set targets.

Trust is also needed but this is difficult to define, despite us knowing when it is there or not. Trust usually needs to be earned and also works together with integrity and honesty. The key ingredients of trust are as follows:

- creditability;
- dependability;

- honesty;
- admitting mistakes;
- openness;
- willingness to listen;
- sharing information;
- giving accurate feedback.

Managers are still be required to give people support; many managers forget that this needed, but giving support is so often the key differentiator between good and normal managers. Support involves giving feedback and assistance in the form of:

- saying thanks;
- listening;
- questioning;
- challenging thinking;
- giving feedback;
- coaching;
- development.

CONTROLLING vs. EMPOWERING

Empowerment has been seen as affecting the culture, values and job design (Source: ACAS *Effective Organisations* booklet), as follows:

- *Culture*
  - In control the emphasis is on rules and procedures with precedent providing guidelines, whereas empowerment emphasises core values with mission statements providing guidance.
  - Emphasis on control and compliance, coordination and control via rules and procedures, versus an emphasis on commitment, coordination and commitment via shared goals, values and traditions.
  - Power and decision making centralised at the top (position authority) versus power and decision making devolved throughout organisation (relevant expertise).
  - Top-down controls (authoritarian) versus mutual influence systems (participative).
  - A culture of inferiority; people cause problems and therefore have to be controlled – versus a culture of pride that will tap into people's problem-solving skills and where people are seen as the greatest asset.
  - Individuality suppressed and systems dominant – the one best way is the system – versus individuals are trusted and can question systems, therefore there is an opportunity to find an appropriate way.
  - Human resource issues are secondary considerations, versus human resource issues are a primary concern in strategic business decisions.
  - A closed system, highly resistant to change, stressing stability, versus an open flexible system, stressing adaptability.
  - Internal orientation, boundary problems and demarcations, versus an external orientation, market led, close to the customer and the environment.

- *Values*
  - Labour is a direct cost to be reduced or eliminated, versus people are an asset to be developed and a major stakeholder in the organisation.
  - People are sources of error, of human failing, versus people are unique, talented flexible resources.
  - People are essentially lazy and try to avoid work, versus people want to take pride in their work and to be productive.
  - People are motivated purely by economic reasons, versus people have a need for recognition, enhanced self-image and influence on the decisions affecting their workspace.
  - Management has to think for the people and closely control and supervise their behaviour, versus management empowers workers to participate in decisions and contribute to personal and organisational growth.

- *Job design*
  - Single tasks, narrow skills, de-skilling and fragmentation, versus grouped tasks requiring multiple broad skills.
  - Laid-down rules and external controls, versus a degree of self-determination.
  - Workers work and managers think, versus combined doing and thinking, everyone's ideas contribute to the company.
  - Fixed job descriptions, versus flexible job descriptions.
  - Quality inspected all at the end, versus everyone responsible for quality.
  - Individuals have no authority, versus individuals encouraged to take decisions and to solve problems.

MANAGEMENT STYLE IN ORGANISATIONS IS IMPORTANT

We have shown briefly above all of the key aspects that are needed to develop effective management practice that will promote good people relationships at work.

Management guides and directs how individuals work together. It fosters good relationships and determines the internal relationships. Without an integrated, coordinated and controlled internal supply chain, then external supply chain management is going to be problematic and at best sub-optimal.

3 *Supply Chain Relationships in Business*

Managing a dependant process in isolation and managing it independently is plain folly. The supply chain is a process; therefore managing it without the collaboration of the other players is a fruitless strategy. But it will be hard for many to make the paradigm shift that is needed to collaborate and to adopt new ways of working.

The authors: Blinding-glimpse-of-the-obvious realisation (April 2005)

We believe that SCM is a philosophy and not a functional department; we also believe that collaboration reduces uncertainty. So in this part of the book we examine internal company structures and how these direct relationships.

We start with a fictional dialogue to link with the first two parts of the book and then continue by noting that power is rooted in structures. Centralised and decentralised structures are compared and differences highlighted; politics and power balances are explored.

We then look at supplier relationships and compare and contrast the traditional adversarial approaches where single goals rule with the collaborative approaches where common goals rule. Changing the approach is also briefly commented on here, it being covered more fully in Part 4.

Supplier appraisal, selection and vendor rating are next examined along with corporate social responsibility (CSR) and supplier audits.

Problems in intercompany relationships and buyer/seller paradigms are discussed next along with the need for re-thinking in SCM. This means attitude change is needed as well as changes to strategy and operations.

Sustaining strategic supplier collaboration and the dynamics of building supply chain relationships are discussed finally in the section on supply chain relationships in business.

Percy and Charlie

As a bridge between the first two parts of this book and the direction we are now heading, consider the following fictional, but very real dialogue:

MR PERCY PROCUREMENT:
But all of this collaboration stuff is just another of those 'new flavour of the month' ideas.

MR CHARLIE COLLABORATION
Well if you were to try something new, maybe you will get something new back in return?
As for being a 'flavour of the month', the question is, what flavour do you want to taste?

PERCY: *A flavour that ensures procurement will get the best deal for our organisation from suppliers. I do not see that collaboration will do this.*

CHARLIE: *Well of course we are always after the best value that meets our business needs, but why can't we get this with collaboration? Why do you assume we cannot get better with collaboration?*

PERCY: *I agree we need value but we don't have time for all of that relationship building and for being nice with suppliers.*

CHARLIE: *Do you have no time for relationship building and being nice with anyone then? I assume by being nice, you mean having good relationships. Surely good relationships are important with everyone and, if so, why should we treat suppliers differently?*
            The question you also really need to ask is, what value can collaboration add to your business?

PERCY: *But I'm happy with what I do now and I do get best value. Suppliers get nothing past me!*

CHARLIE: *I am sure they do not and I am very sure you get nothing from them either!*

PERCY: *Eh, such as?*

CHARLIE: *Well it is always good to talk and to listen and to share. In this way you can explore mutual interests. After all, don't they also want best value for themselves?*
            So, what if you found a way of giving them something like sales forecast information, so that it made their work easier so that, in turn, they would give something more back to you?

PERCY: *Sounds to be getting complicated to me, anyway, we could never give them confidential information.*

CHARLIE: *Yes, this can be an issue, it really goes with trust. If you can't trust your suppliers then don't do it. But I suspect you already do trust them anyway*

PERCY: *Well yes we trust them, I suppose, to deliver on time the correct quality products, and if they don't, we penalise them.*

CHARLIE: *Well that is what is called contractual trust. Hold onto this trust idea, we are making some headway!*
            A question, if you penalise them does this sometimes mean getting rid of them?

PERCY: *Sure, if they don't meet our standards, then we look for someone else. We are continually looking for alternatives and try to have at least one alternative supplier waiting in the wings.*

CHARLIE: *Well I am sure examining alternative supplier sourcing is always going to be important for some of products, like your bottleneck items. But, could I just say that on your critical items, replacement suppliers may not be available. It is probably only your routine items that can be viewed as being easily replaceable.*

Remember that most suppliers are like cogs in the machine and losing a supplier can cost you your production, sales and customers. What you really need to appreciate, Percy, is that harnessing the supplier's knowledge can add value to both businesses

PERCY: *But this is all going to involve a whole new way of thinking. Why bother and why change?*

CHARLIE: *Well I have not said it was easy. But what makes it a necessity is that the old ways of doing things will only last until such time as a competitor comes along who has initiated an improved way; like collaboration that harnesses the creative talent of both the suppliers and customers in the supply chain.*

PERCY: *But our industry is different surely?*

CHARLIE: *Let's look at some examples of people who felt they were different and special and immune.*

As examples in manufacturing, look at the current UK car and electronics industries and the extent that that some of these companies have been off-shored in the process.

Some changed; some have not and have effectively vanished from the market (Rover cars and NCR to name just two).

We can also see similar patterns from the retail sector; consider former 'number one' companies like Sainsbury's and Marks & Spencer who have been overtaken by their competitors, Tesco and Asda/George – both of which have more up-to-date SCM practices as well as better product development and other aspects.

Tesco, for example, heavily has invested in distribution centre networks and IT systems infrastructure since the early 1990s, but Sainsbury's only came round to this in the late 1990s and subsequently had serious implementation issues in 2004.

Asda/George for example has SCM and replenishment as a key strategy and, along with Tesco, sells more clothes than Marks & Spencer. Marks & Spencer also had well-documented supply problems with suppliers when they offshored production.

Percy, the competition will view your comments of 'we are different' as a blocker for you but as an enabler for them!

No doubt this type of debate is familiar to many readers as it is to us. The next two parts of this book will further examine such issues and how they can be positively overcome.

Internal structures and relationships

Power is rooted in the internal organisation structure of organisations. Power is found in:

- the position and styles of the people (for example, autocratic, charismatic);
- the control of resources;
- the knowledge held.

Power ranges on the organisation structure continuum from power existing in centralised command-and-control mechanical structures, at one end, to the more open decentralised matrix organic structures with devolved and delegated power, at the opposite end.

The distinctions between structures reveal important differences; for example with procurement:

Centralised procurement structures	Decentralised procurement structures
Bulk buy and place large orders	Smaller fragmented orders
Specialists are located together	Generalists are found
Suppliers have single point of contact	Suppliers have many points of contact
Distant from users/customers	Nearer to users/customers
'Ivory tower' syndrome	More hands-on controls
Inflexible to change to suit localised conditions	Easily adapt to local conditions

POLITICS

Many organisations are unfortunately full of playground politics that add no value to either the individuals or to the organisation. Here blame culture rules.

If you spend time in the company of any organisation, then you pick up on the conversations and the feelings of the people working there.

Sadly this is often 'moaning and groaning' and covers topics from the earlier-mentioned dissatisfier factors of Herzburg, such as:

- company policy/administration; for example, 'have you heard what they are doing now';
- supervision; for example, 'Mr Smith has no idea';
- working conditions; for example, 'the canteen here is terrible';
- personal relationships; for example, 'I think Mrs Jones is awful';
- salary/pay/benefits; 'the pay here is poor'.

Comments like the above in an organisation can reveal the practical inadequacy of the organisation's vision where, for example, the mission statement has remained mere theory. This may be despite the efforts of some in the organisation to promote the mission statement, believing that it will make a real difference.

It can be that those at the top that are often camouflaged and protected from seeing the practical realities of their policy statements. Mission statements rarely become significant in such an organisation.

People are individuals and need to function at this level. They may not be impacted by global collective mission statements – these may not be explained meaningfully to these individuals, the very ones who are actually expected to take the mission statement forward

POWER BALANCES

Whilst it is generally recognised that building closer relationships with customers and suppliers through a collaborative supply chain is desirable and produces benefits for all parties involved in practice, many questions are raised however.

What if, for example, the company with which you are trying to develop a relationship is much larger or smaller than your own? How do you ensure that everybody in both organisations works to the new style of trading and not to a confrontational traditional style? How do you build trust when there may be many historical reasons for fear to exist?

The key conclusion is that the focus on a single goal of collaboration is unrealistic. A focus on this to the exclusion of other possibilities may be depriving companies of many valuable benefits that can be derived from other levels of supply chain integration. Service to the end customer can be driven to even higher standards by focusing the whole supply chain on that goal, rather than diluting the efforts of individual companies through conflicting objectives.

Companies that have succeeded in integrating supply chains have achieved breakthrough improvements. For example, in consumer products an integrated approach between a manufacturer and retailer resulted in sales doubling over five years, with supply chain costs cut by 25 per cent and inventory almost eliminated. In the clothing industry, strategies integrating all stages in the supply chain have increased sales by up to 20 per cent, halved inventories and reduced markdowns on end-of-line stock by more than 33 per cent.

Many companies and commentators have thought in terms of building collaborative partnerships, but this ideal is not easily achieved where there is an atmosphere of suspicion resulting from previous behaviour. This has caused many to hold back.

Consequently, these companies are faced with the challenge of continuing to find revenue, cost and service improvements based on internal actions alone. However, this is not a route for achieving the required levels of competitiveness. So, there is clearly a need for an improved understanding of the relationships between customer and supplier.

The use and abuse of power plays a formative role when integrating supply chains. The power created by the size or dominance of one of the organisations involved in the supply chain is not diminished because the company chooses to build closer relationships with suppliers and customers. Companies however will need to recognise that the relationship will be driven by the relative power and interdependence of the parties involved.

Many companies are working from models and caricatures of power and there are also those companies striving for caricatures of collaboration and partnerships. Therefore, understanding the power a company has and more importantly the power it can gain by acting differently is the starting point for structuring the portfolio of relationships needed.

The organisations must understand their positions in the supply chain and each must be in the position to maximise benefits in the context of the whole chain. Only then can the collective power of all companies in that chain be focused on competing in the marketplace, one supply chain against another.

Companies may recognise that the collaboration ideal can be exactly that, an ideal, and not a prerequisite. The level and features of the relationship must be appropriate to the mutual interests of all the companies involved. By tailoring each relationship, based on recognition of the interests and fears of all parties involved, a new source of breakthrough improvement can becomes available.

It seems very clear that closer relationships between suppliers and customers will become a competitive necessity. But caution is needed, as a naïve belief in an ill-defined concept of collaborative and partnership as a universal panacea will do more harm than good. A new realism is required when looking to integrate supply chains with collaborative relationships; a realism that considers the practical difficulties of integration, the level of sophistication of the participants and the nature of competitive advantage and power within the supply chain.

There is no single one-size-fits-all solution for all customers or suppliers. Integration approaches must be tailored to the needs and the capabilities of each party involved. Each company will therefore have a different mix or portfolio of supply chain relationships with each operating at different levels. The key is to select the right one for the right supply chain.

TYPES OF SUPPLIER RELATIONSHIPS

These may be briefly described as follows:

Relationship	Supply base	Methods
Arm's length	Multiple sourcing	Competitive tendering and spot buying
Cooperative	Fewer suppliers	Negotiation and preferred suppliers with framework agreements
Collaborative	Possible single sourcing	Open book
Partnership	Single sourcing	Joint working towards continuous improvements

Related to the procurement portfolio, the following is the position between sellers and buyers/ suppliers and customers:

Bottleneck	**Critical/strategic**
Supplier: power Customer: dependence on seller Buyer is slave to/hostage of the seller	Supplier: interdependence Customer: interdependence Buyer: interdependence
Routine	**Leverage**
Supplier: trader Customer: trades Buyer: trading	Supplier: dependant on buyer Customer: power Buyer is master with a servant seller

The change from more arm's-length transactional relationships to more collaborative relationships can also reflect a move towards more adaptive supply chains. This makes for an interesting comparison and an 'ideal-typical' comparison follows:

Transactional relationships	Collaboration relationships
Contracts with suppliers	
Short term	Long term
Multi-sourcing	Single sourcing
Distant and contractual relationships	Close and collaborative relationships
Little commitment beyond the contract	Involvement and 'shared destiny'
Information exchanged is orders	Information is shared including forward strategy
Trust is not needed	Trust is essential
Style is competitive, win/lose, power base is combative with command/control behaviour	Style is collaborative, win/win, power base is non existent with honest, open and truthful (HOT) behaviour
Price/risk	
Price orientation	Total cost of ownership
Price dominates	Shared destiny dominates
One way	Two-way exchanges
Customer demands sensitive data	Exchanges of sensitive data
Customer keeps all cost savings	Mutual efforts to reduce costs, times and waste
All risk with supplier, the buyer risks little	Shared risk and benefits
'What is in it for me'	'What is in it for us'
Short term	Long term
Negotiations	
Strong use of ploys in negotiations	Mutual gains rule discussions
Power based	Equality based
Win/lose	Win/win
'One-off' deals	'Forever' together
Walk in and out of, change is easy	Difficult to break, change is difficult
Easy to set up	Difficult to set up
Adversarial and maybe inefficient for one party	Challenging to implement and continue with
'Partnershaft'	Partnership
Interpersonal relationships	
No personal relationships	Strong personal relationship
Separated/arm's length	Close/alliance
Low contact/closed	Shared vision/open
Predatory power based	Proactive and more people based
Hierarchical/superior subordinate	Equality
Blame culture	Problem-solving gain culture
Alienated employees	Motivated employees
Trust	
Trust is based on what the contract says (contractual trust)	Trust is based on goodwill, commitment and cooperation
Little ongoing trust	Continual trust plus risk/benefits sharing
Power-based spin	Pragmatic tough trust
Controls	
Strong on tactical/ departmental controls	Strong on marketing strategy and supply chain alignment
High formal controls	Self-controlled
Rigid contracts	Flexible contracts
Technical performance and the specifications rule	Work beyond just one technical view
Resource and capacity capabilities	Mutual long-term capabilities
Measure by non compliance	Both measure and agree remedial action

The change from transactional methods to collaborative approaches goes far beyond the technical issues of say ICT connectivity and fully embraces the soft skills.

The view and belief here from sponsors of collaborative approaches is that if all players worked well together that a lot more would get done, more efficiently and more effectively. The evidence for this from basic relationship principles is overwhelming. However, many people will not subscribe to such a mutually sharing collaborative SCM approach.

A major reason for not doing this is the belief that business and the buying/selling activity is founded on power: two-way collaboration is an uneasy concept; it is easier in one-way power-based transactions to beat up and exert influence.

Another reason for not recognising or pursuing collaborative relationships is that the needed applications of soft skills are actually the hard skills for many people in business. Indeed, SCM collaboration between companies is unlikely to succeed without appropriate recognition that soft-skill development is required.

Collaborative relationships depend on trust. Without trust, there is no relationship. If businesses are not prepared to trust each other, then collaboration relationships will not work and should not be attempted.

Collaboration needs to have some basic principles and the rules of collaboration are:

- Real and recognised benefits must be found for all involved internal and external players.
- Integrate business processes at all stages.
- Gain support from all of the supply chain components.
- Recognise the different cultures involved.
- Correct people relationships are needed and, when improving people relationships, it is useful to remember that:
  - It is the soft stuff that is the hard stuff.
  - People may be physically present, but are they there psychologically?
  - Only when all people come together is found the power of one.

Preventing achievement of the above benefits are the barriers to collaboration, such as the following:

Barriers	Comments
No trust	The fear here is usually of giving information that will be made available to the competition or used against the providers
Poor communications	This usually means there is no up-to-date sharing and also this makes a comment on the format of communication being used
No big picture view	Too focused on own issues and problems
No risk taking	Fear of having all eggs in one basket and a preference for 'playing off'
Prefer power-based adversary transactional approach	Annual contracts and three quotes, common in the public sector, continues to perpetuate adversary approaches
Want quick and short-term wins	In reality success will depend on time and effort over longer periods
No sharing of benefits	The power view of keeping it all, whereas all should save from mutual collaborations
No planning, all kick and rush	Collaboration is hard work involving soft skills. It also will need adequate planning

Barriers	Comments
No support for any changing 'how we do things'	Top support is important
'Output is king and anyway, we are too busy fire-fighting'	Concentration here is on the operations and looking just for short-term efficiency whilst ignoring longer-term effectiveness.
Fear of change	Remaining with the status quo in times of change and stable turbulence that is akin to the ostrich analogy of burying the head in the sand.
Fear of failure from the existing blame culture	Change to a gain culture is needed.

What fundamentally has to be changed to bring in collaborative supply chain relationships are first, people, then the following:

- contracts to simple flexible approaches;
- intensive management involvement;
- periodic performance monitoring;
- internal controls for confidential information;
- problem-solving procedures;
- supplier is seen as a customer;
- cross-functional supplier/customer teams;
- hub (supply chain managers) and spoke (suppliers/customer) organisations;
- and people last, as people change one at a time. It is people that change a company and it is the people who make the relationships in and between companies.

Changing the company culture ('what is done around here') will involve passing through the following stages (of course not all companies will be starting out by having to change from a blame culture so for some companies the transition will be easier):

Aspect	Stormy/blame culture	Steady/sane culture	Sunny/gain culture
Goals	Announced	Communicated	Agreed
Information	Status symbol and power based	Traded	Abundant
Motivation	Manipulative	Focused on staff needs	A clear goal
Decisions	From above	Partly delegated	Staff take them
Mistakes	Are only made by staff	Responsibility is taken	Are allowed as learning lessons
Conflicts	Are unwelcome and 'put down'	Are mastered	Source of new innovation
Control	From above	Partly delegated	Fully delegated
Management style	Authoritarian/aggressive	Cooperative	Participative/assertive
Authority	Requires obedience	Requires cooperation	Requires collaboration
Manager	Absolute ruler and feels superior	Problem solver and decision maker	Change strategist and self-confident

Supplier appraisal

Now let us focus on the very important task of selecting and measuring suppliers and contractors in order to assess those more suitable for potential long-term collaboration. This is a process known as supplier appraisal, which is then followed by vendor rating and quality audits.

The whole ethos of this book is based on the premise that collaboration will bring benefits. However, before building close collaborative ventures, it is of course, imperative to look consistently at the supplier base by using supplier appraisal criteria. Done correctly, this can be far reaching and beyond simply looking at what is the lowest price.

Accordingly, clients should be looking at a range of evidence in several key areas, which together completed the jigsaw of supplier appraisal. The following looks at two major models being used currently.

APPROVAL CRITERIA

Many government departments have now adopted this approach to supplier appraisal. When seeking to approve suppliers, procurement departments must be satisfied that as a minimum they are:

- technically sound
- managerially competent
- adequately resourced
- financially stable
- reliable.

Therefore, organisations must have tangible evidence of achievement and success in these areas. We will now look at each of these key criteria in greater detail.

Technically sound and technically competent

To be technically sound, suppliers/contractors must demonstrate technical competence as measured below:

- technical background, training and experience of key personnel;
- organisation and control of technical activities; for example, estimating, design, procurement, installation;
- quality assurance standards applicable and methods of implementation;
- familiarity with industry standards;
- availability of testing equipment and procedures;
- adequacy of after-sales service, availability and location of service engineers, spare parts, response time;
- record on innovation and quality improvement – continuous improvement in design and specifications is part of their normal working culture;
- record on environmental systems.

When adequately resourced, can they actually cope with the volume and quantity of work which a company can offer? Can they provide the following:

- adequate dimensions of workshops and machine tools availability;
- appropriate numbers and skill levels of manufacturing/personnel;
- adequate logistics system, for example, warehouses, transport;
- proven production planning and control systems;
- packaging and shipping facilities;
- details of work generally subcontracted or bought in, including names of suppliers.

Managerially competent

How well run is the company?

- Organisation of company – availability of detailed organisation charts and staff numbers.
- Overall corporate structure (where company is a subsidiary).
- Key management policies covering training, career development and so on.
- Availability of job descriptions for key staff.
- Safety policy of company and record over say last three years.
- Maximum size and complexity of contract that can be efficiently managed.

Financial stability

Even quality companies can go bankrupt unless their finances are strong. Ensure:

- copies of the last two annual reports are available;
- bankers' references are available;
- you have an independent reference; for example commercial sector companies (Dun and Bradstreet);
- parent company prepared to guarantee formally the performance of the subsidiary;
- company is prepared to furnish performance bonds.

Reliability

Nowadays, clients want consistency of conforming output every time. Therefore, can suppliers demonstrate reliability?

- Customer service record of meeting delivery/completion dates, supported by a record on late deliveries/completion dates with reasons and names of customers affected.
- Service factor – equipment downtime.
- Availability of planned maintenance.

Vendor rating

Vendor rating measures an existing supplier's performance. This relates to the manner in which it carries out its total obligations against a purchase order/contract from the time it is instructed to proceed with it. A supplier's performance may be compared with:

- a standard;
- performance on a previous order;
- another supplier's performance.

Advantages of using vendor rating are as follows:

- Any identified weaknesses on the part of the supplier can be addressed or concessions/compensation sought for poor performance.
- The data may be used to evaluate and compare performances of new suppliers.
- Vendor rating acts as a controlling tool of performance.
- Measurement can be used as the basis of continuous improvement.
- Measurement on a two-way basis can highlight the buyer's deficiencies (which may be the source of common problems across many supplier relationships).
- Objective and subjective measurements give an overall picture of the supplier's/buyer's performance.
- Each company gains a better understanding of the constraints, deadlines, potential and so on that affect the relationship.
- It removes emotive issues such as personal relationships between buyer and supplier.

CASE STUDY
BORG INSTRUMENTS

Borg Instruments' buyers, using a special formula, convert vendors' monthly performance ratings into cash values. They add these amounts to supplier's bids as handicaps or 'fines'. The poorer a supplier's performance rating, the higher the bid handicap he gets.

To illustrate, a supplier with a semi-annual score of 94 points has a penalty factor of 6 per cent: their bid is inflated by 6 per cent. If their bid was £1000 it is raised to £1060. The supplier with the lowest bid may lose the business if its penalty is significantly higher than those of its competitors.

Borg's vendor rating system rewards good performance, helps eliminate marginal suppliers and is a defence against the occasional vendor who bids low to 'buy' business, intending to recoup later by relaxing on quality. Monthly ratings permit buyers to detect waning quality almost as soon as it develops. They can take prompt, effective action.

(*Source*: 'Use of Bid Handicaps to Stimulate Supplier Performance', Borg Instruments case study, www.cips.org)

CASE STUDY
BRITISH GAS

The following is a summary list of the main principles of the 'Golden Torch for Quality of Service and Excellence' that was used by British Gas to assess its appliance manufacturer's suppliers:

All the requirements for quality are defined as criteria and each criterion is measured by those employees closest to that activity (called criterion owners).

Bullet-point lists detail what is expected for a supplier to achieve a perfect score.

Criterion owners meet monthly to score and feed back each supplier's performance.

A spreadsheet calculates total scores and publishes a league table.

Each supplier sees its own detailed performance and the league table.

The Golden Torch is used in purchasing decisions, especially when deciding upon a shortlist for potential collaboration. There are six-monthly formal reviews and the criteria are reviewed annually.

The mix of measurement techniques used to score the criteria is limited to three:

* yes/no measure where possible;
* subjective measure on an A–E basis;
* calculated measure as a percentage, for example:

Criterion	Measure	%
Stock appliance deliveries	A-E	16
Special order appliances	%	8
Stock spares deliveries	%	12
Special order spares	%	8
Sales office relationship	A–E	12
Goods inwards relationship	A–E	8
Use of EDI	Y/N	4
Defective goods	A–E	8
Delivery performance	Y/N	8
Provision of initial spares	A–E	4
Opening hours	Y/N	4
Packaging and labelling	A–E	4
Accuracy of invoices	A–E	4
Total		100

Corporate social responsibility

A buyer can make corporate social responsibility (CSR) to be a condition of working with a supplier and can therefore be a part of a buyer's supplier appraisal. Few people would disagree with the principal aims of CSR:

- protecting children in developing countries against exploitation;
- ensuring health and safety;
- protecting the environment.

These are issues important to everyone. For purchasers in small- and medium-sized enterprises, the challenge will be even more daunting. Being told to find out what your suppliers are doing about corporate responsibility is a thoroughly laudable objective but for many may seem a huge challenge.

Let's say you are a company with 4000 suppliers and have a procurement team of 15. This means that each of your professional purchasers handles an average of 266 suppliers. A CSR audit might take a day for each supplier. That means the purchasing team will be spending all its operational time and more on CSR compliance. This may be an entirely theoretical example, but for many the task will appear impossible.

There are ways of checking suppliers' bona fides without spending huge amounts of valuable time on it. Methods of accessing information on suppliers are becoming increasingly sophisticated. They can now take account not just of financial status, reliability, quality standards and so on, but also whether suppliers conform to minimum standards on health and safety, people developments, pay and conditions, environmental good practice and all the other factors that go towards a CSR policy.

ETHICS AND CSR

Around the world, millions of adults and children in developing countries are working in conditions that compromise their fundamental human rights. Should the buying company care? If the organisation buys from the developing world or if their suppliers do, then yes it should. As purchasers who live in affluent, democratic nations, we surely have a moral obligation to ensure that our decisions do not support those governments, companies or individuals whose actions abuse human rights.

There are a number of arguments that are commonly made against this point of view, for example:

> *My responsibility is to my shareholders. I cannot let ethical or moral issues interfere in my consideration of value for money. And if I didn't buy from these companies, my competitors would. The workers would still be exploited and we would be at a competitive disadvantage.*

> *Developing countries depend on international trade. Take it away and their workforce would be worse off.*

> *Forcing developing economies to operate to the employment standards of the developed world makes their industry uncompetitive.*

> *Who do we think we are to force our opinions, standards and beliefs on other nations?*

Certainly, from the viewpoint of the procurement manager, 'globalisation' means being able to source supplies from wherever in the world there is the best combination of quality, price, service, communications, administrative capabilities and total cost.

As a consequence, new and enhanced skills are needed to plan and manage the total supply and value chain from an ethical and corporate social responsibility standpoint.

Too often, globalisation tends to be a pejorative term covering anything about the US, an international organisation such as the World Trade Organisation, or multinational business. However, globalisation is really about the freedom to trade throughout the world, while respecting individuals' right to life, liberty, employment, security and the ongoing health of the environment.

The question of whether a moral obligation exists between companies and those who work in their supply chains is extremely complex. Consumers are outraged by stories of children working for pennies to produce desirable consumer goods that retail in the West for tens or even hundreds of pounds. When confronted by what they perceive to be exploitation, they often react by refusing to buy products from organisations that are deemed to have transgressed. For example, a fall in Nike's sales and profits was attributed to resistance by consumers because of persistent allegations that the company mistreats its factory workers. Similarly, when Manchester United were found buying football shirts at very low prices from regions that were later found to be using child labour, the negative publicity was not welcomed by the club, who had to tighten up their purchasing policies.

What then can be done to manage this risk?

Remember, that a company can only be considered ethical (with corporate social responsibility), if all of the suppliers, contractors and intermediaries in the supply chain are ethical and socially responsible. The first step is to discover just where the procurement spends actually go; for example, are you sure that you know the origin of all the direct products you buy? Are you aware of the suppliers or markets from which your direct suppliers source their materials? This must form part of normal supplier appraisal, which we have just examined above.

There are a number of alternatives. The first is to work with specific suppliers to improve the working conditions of particular groups of employees. However, this is time consuming and resource intensive. Businesses might therefore decide to develop a company code of conduct for social accountability. Indeed many have already. According to a report by the Overseas Development Administration, Tesco, Unilever, ICI, Sainsbury's, Shell, Clark's Shoes and BAT have all taken this route. The report recommends that company codes should, at the very minimum, address the core conventions of the International Labour Organisation on forced labour, freedom of association, collective bargaining, minimum age of workers, discrimination and equal remuneration.

However, company codes of conduct may not represent the best way forward for social accountability. Alice Tipper Marlin, president of the US Council on Economic Priorities (CEP), says: 'Companies find it extremely difficult to deliver on and verify corporate responsibility when dealing with a network of hundreds or even thousands of vendors, contractors and suppliers.' Internal codes are expensive and inefficient, since laws and customs vary widely and contracting companies regard their sources and audits as proprietary. Often, it is difficult for those companies to get reliable information. Factory owners, in turn, are taxed by having to undergo multiple audits to differing sets of standards, each with its own requirements and paperwork. Internal systems by their nature are neither transparent nor independently verified, resulting in credibility problems instead of solutions.

CEP's alternative to single company codes of conduct is called Social Accountability 8000 (SA 8000) which is modelled on the international quality standard ISO 9000.

It is intended that companies will apply for SA 8000 in the same way that they might apply for ISO 9000. To qualify, they will have to submit to a rigorous audit/accreditation process. For successful applicants, accreditation will last for three years with surveillance audits conducted every six months.

By specifying SA 8000, it is hoped that customer organisations will be able to demonstrate the integrity of their supply chains. It is also expected that the momentum in the developing world to achieve SA 8000 will have a positive impact on improving working conditions for large numbers of individuals, without putting their livelihoods at risk.

A number of organisations, including Toys R Us, are reported to be requiring all their suppliers to adopt SA 8000. Other organisations have made commitments to require their key suppliers to adopt the standard.

Some might question whether such a system will prove effective. How many purchasers, for example, would rely solely on ISO 9000 to assure supplier quality? Others might question specific provisions within its code, but SA 8000 and similar initiatives cannot be ignored.

Organisations must remember that consumers as well as their business-to-business trade customers are more likely to be using evidence of an ethical approach when deciding upon a buying decision. Therefore, although there may be initial costs involved to improve the ethical position of the supply chain, in the long term it is good for business as well as being morally and ethically correct.

CORPORATE SOCIAL RESPONSIBLY AND BUSINESS SENSE

Right across the world, companies are recognising the clear business benefits of adopting a socially responsible approach.

A UK survey in 2001 found that about 80 per cent of FTSE 100 companies provide information about their environmental performance, social impact or both. A growing number of companies of all sizes are finding that there are business benefits from being socially responsible.

Dr Steve New of the Said Business School, Oxford, believes purchasing professionals have a crucial role to play in making their companies behave more ethically. 'Many organisations act on criteria that are not purely commercial. Most purchasers take into account such things as quality, improving delivery times and product development when working with suppliers. These are the same sort of criteria that can be used to bring improvements on ethical issues.'

Dr New points to three major reasons for the upsurge of interest in ethical behaviour:

- The arrival of mass global communication, which has made the behaviour of a company on one side of the world visible to its customers on the other.
- Organisations are more concerned about risk management, particularly in terms of legislation. Corporations are beginning to realise that what is just about acceptable business practice now may not be so in the future not just in terms of public approbation but also legally.
- People are thinking through the moral consequences of the idea that organisations include their entire chain of production.

Dr New continues, 'If suppliers and distributors are in some sense part of the core organisation and companies feel some responsibility for coordinating them, then it logically follows that they must have some responsibility for moral and ethical issues.'

Certainly, the UK Chartered Institute of Purchasing and Supply (CIPS) believes its members can take the social responsibility agenda further. It has published its code on ethical business practices to include guidelines not only on personal behaviour but also a section on 'Social Responsibility'. It sets out comprehensive objectives in such areas as employment, rights, freedom of association, wages, health and safety, child labour and discrimination.

The Institute's 'Ethical practices in purchasing and supply' draws on various codes, including the UK government-backed Ethical Trading initiative, the core conventions of the International Labour Organisation and the UN Declaration on Human Rights. It says purchasers should work with suppliers to make sure that:

- Employees are free to choose whether or not to work for their employer.
- Employees should be given a clear contract, including how much they will be paid.
- Suppliers should not discourage or prevent employees from joining trade unions.
- Wages and benefits should at least meet industry benchmarks or national legal standards.
- Employees should not be expected to work more than 48 hours a week regularly.
- Suppliers should not abuse or intimidate employees.
- Suppliers should always work within the laws of their country.
- Suppliers should uphold health and safety requirements.

They aim to eradicate child labour, but in the meantime make sure children and your people are not made to work in dangerous conditions or at night, and that they have access to education.

(The full text of the code is available from the CIPS website at: www.cips.org/about/policies.asp)

Supplier audits

In order to ensure continuous improvement in a close working collaboration relationship, it is essential to measure the ongoing performance in order to establish action plans that will ensure mutuality in terms of shared risk and shared reward.

The following section portrays an example of such an approach in terms of quality audits.

Supplier auditing is a time-consuming activity that needs to have clearly defined objectives if it is to have value to a business. In the traditional supplier–customer relationship, the audit often seems to be used as a way of finding as many faults as possible in the way the supplier operates, in order to provide a negotiating lever.

In collaborative customer–supplier relationships where the supplier is regarded as a partner rather than someone to be exploited, the role of the quality auditor is one of adviser, identifying areas for improvement for mutual benefit.

Such improvement is not limited to product quality issues but can also involve lead times, on-time delivery and service. It is also not a one-sided process. There may be opportunities for improvement in the way the customer communicates with the supplier for instance. This is the approach which Hewlett-Packard Fibre Optic Components Operation, Ipswich, UK has adopted in carrying out assessments of its suppliers. The auditor's role is to identify areas for improvement in the trading basis between Hewlett-Packard and its supplier. Meaningless procedures, just for the sake of bureaucracy, have no place in the relationship since they add cost for the supplier which will inevitably be passed on to the customer in some form. The goal here is improvements.

A typical audit will begin with an overview of the quality management system, in which the auditor gets to understand the organisation and documentation used by the audited company. The auditor then begins a walk through of the supplier's order fulfilment process.

In reviewing the way in which orders are received, it is often possible to identify areas for improvement in the way in which requirements are communicated to the supplier. This has led to improvement actions being taken back by the auditor to be actioned within Hewlett-Packard. One example was the fact that suppliers often found that the Hewlett-Packard Procurement Department had not supplied them with the latest issue of the specification, so they might not have been working to the correct drawing.

The auditor's aim is to draw a balanced picture of the operation of the supplier and to identify areas where improvement would benefit the supplier and the customer.

The auditor will also look at the supplier's system for internal quality audits and corrective/preventative action. The internal quality audit is the supplier's own tool for measuring the effectiveness of their quality system. Corrective and preventative actions are the improvement process that closes the loop to prevent recurrence of problems, whether highlighted by customers or the supplier's own investigations.

The name of the game is to get the supplier thinking about how they can make their operation more efficient, doing things right first time, at minimum cost. The expectation is that the cost savings will be shared with the customer.

The payback should come in the improved understanding of each company's requirements that develops from the audit process, which then facilitates a deeper level of collaboration.

Structuring for supply chain management

As we have noted earlier, SCM is all about integrating and coordinating both internal and external independent processes so that there is inter-dependency that reduces uncertainty due to the reliability of flows of goods and information/money. We have also noted that power is rooted in the structure of companies.

So the question arises, how do we structure for effective SCM?

The first (and in fact the last point) on SCM structures in organisations is that SCM is not a division, department or a section. It is therefore not another structural silo to be bolted on to existing departments of production, procurement, logistics, marketing, finance and so on.

SCM is cross-functional; it therefore needs to be organised this way.

Also, SCM is a philosophy, like TQM (total quality management). For TQM to be successful then quality must exist and be recognised throughout the company. Similarly, SCM must exist and have recognition in all the parts and processes of a business. Just as 'quality' is not owned by a TQM department, similarly the supply chain is not owned by any named SCM department. Giving the SCM process a structure and organisation like any of the other company silo functions will only therefore serve to confuse the purpose of SCM and lead to in-fighting and power plays commonly already found between existing functional silos.

The point here is that the whole business is the supply chain. So everyone owns the supply chain and everyone has responsibility for the successful supply chain mission achievement. This for example is usually that of satisfying the customer (both the internal ones as well as the final one).

SCM in company structure terms can be equated with a matrix project management structure, with the supply chain horizontally cutting across all the vertically managed functional silos. Having such a matrix-based structure, may mean that SCM 'signs off' the production plans, determines stock levels and overall acts as 'the department of trade-offs' and as 'the holistic people'.

Such structuring can therefore mean fundamental and radical changes are needed to existing organisational structures. But without this, how will be the full benefits of SCM be realised?

Ways forward towards such restructuring and re-thinking the business towards SCM practices will need to include internal education and training on what the supply chain is, the course programme participants being all the appropriate internal members of an organisation. The following content is one example of such an education course.

SUPPLY CHAIN EDUCATION

Session 1: Understanding what the supply chain is about

- definitions of SCM;
- the interrelations and connections of buying, making, moving, and selling activities;
- history and development;
- a view of the future.

Session 2: Key aspects of SCM

- the cost/service balance;
- customer service principles;
- lead times;
- adding value;
- production options/changes;
- trade-off opportunities;

Session 3: Benefits of adopting an SCM approach

- understanding the sub-functional conflicts;
- benefits within and between functions;
- taking a supply chain view of total acquisition costs.

Session 4: Why SCM will change traditional ways

- looking at demand amplifications, and the 'Forrester Effect';
- appreciating the effects of uncertainty and unresponsiveness.

Session 5: Impacts to relationships

- sharing developments;
- eliminating internal and external barriers;
- interfacing versus integrating relationships.

Session 6: Implementing an SCM approach

- the changes needed;
- the 'doing nothing' future;
- breaking down traditional silos/closed management;
- potential action needed.

Outcomes and actions from such training can be where the entire course members design, agree and sign up to an internal SCM campaign statement such as, 'Manage the flow and watch the company grow'. It can also include agreeing to a supply chain vision statement that is used to take the SCM initiative forward. The following is an example:

- The supply chain is not owned by one department.
- The supply chain will only work with cross-functional understanding.
- Our mission is supply chain effectiveness in serving our internal and our external customers.

The wording used here is an example only. The actual words used are of secondary importance to having a shared commitment to the agreed statement.

To encourage cross-functionalism further then, team-based education/training programmes may be used. These programmes can have a negotiated and agreed outcome, as shown in the following example:

We, as a team, committed to the following at place x on date y:

- We will use the right language in all our dealings with others.
- We will be open with each other.
- We will support each other, especially in front of others.
- We will have the confidence to confront each other.
- We will deliver quality work.

This means that we agree to:

- Trust each other.
- Openly share ideas.
- Openly exchange of information.
- Innovate and change.
- Mutual understanding.
- Cost reduction across the supply chain.
- Improved service across the supply chain.

Finally, we will have a common cause, we will trust, we will talk and listen, we will not blame, we are survivors in the same boat.

Signed: by all participants

The use of cross-functional teams is beneficial in bringing change to the supply chain. They can effectively be used to overcome functional blocks and one-sided views. Many departments and functions regard their own work as efficient and the only way that things should be done; meanwhile they see that it is the other departments and functions that get it wrong and are not moving forward.

Cross-functional teams will therefore challenge themselves. The team asks challenging questions about conventional ways of 'how we do things round here': they can challenge directly the work culture. When cross-functional teams are used with external suppliers/customers, then progress can be made up and downstream in the supply chain.

Intercompany relationships

The optimum and the ideal in SCM will only ever be found by working and collaborating fully with all parties. As we earlier noted, the change from transactional methods to collaborative approaches goes far beyond the technical issues of, say, ICT connectivity, and fully embraces the soft skills. SCM collaboration between companies will not succeed without appropriate recognition that soft-skills development is required. This section will examine, albeit briefly, this largely soft-skill area.

Collaborative relationships need to work together towards a common goal. They are based on the principle that each party can gain more benefits by collaboration than by pursuing self-interest at any cost. Companies that are using and realising the benefits of supply chain collaboration have recognised that many key performance objectives, such as profitability and market share are achievable by all supply chain players.

The traditional approach to suppliers was to assume that they were adversaries. Here it was important to let them know as little as possible in case they could gain a price advantage. The best protection was to ensure that each supplier lived under the shadow of an alternative potential source. However, the kind of performance a company needs to achieve in today's competitive markets now requires at least an equal contribution from suppliers. Suppliers cannot perform at this level in an environment of uncertainty.

Consider the following case study; we have italicised the important parts:

CASE STUDY
UK CAR ASSEMBLERS' SUPPLY STRATEGY

The company has a focused product supply strategy that is integrally linked to the philosophy of the 'extended enterprise' where the destinies of suppliers, dealers and workers at every level of the business are inseparable. This is reinforced through promotional and marketing messages that stress the responsibility the company owes to its dealer network. The former chairman had previously and publicly threw down the gauntlet to component suppliers in a bid to make them understand that the company was not a meal ticket. Nowadays, threats are replaced by promises. The following statement from the MD explains their current position:

Our relationship with the supply community today is very pervasive. It is not just about price and output any more, nor has it been for a long time; but it is about culture, management style and about whether the right things are happening within the framework of the business for a particular partner to be someone in whom we can invest a long-term, lifetime partnership relationship. You have to handle it with care.

The company now recognises that a supplier can be a positive partner and a loyal companion while serving different customers, and that having different dialogues can be healthy.

'We have to share the benefits, to understand that you cannot have a lifetime relationship unless the partner is financially healthy, but that achieving this does not introduce a price and cost structure that is uncompetitive to the end product,' the MD says. 'At one time, people would say, "if we do this, it will benefit X, Y and Z as well", but we take the view that you waste a lot of time in that narrow mind-set. *It is more productive to think about the fact that by both of you being involved there is a benefit of shared knowledge and experience, which benefits everyone, in particular your customers.* We have recognised that just because you happen to be the biggest link in the chain, which comprises the extended enterprise, this does not imply superiority. You need to use your facilities, resources and even your philosophical capability to extend processes in all directions, both internally and externally.'

Collaborative relationships therefore create a more secure environment. Relationships become long term, buyers and sellers learn more about each other's business and so the nature of the negotiation undergoes a fundamental change. Price then becomes a matter of open, detailed discussion with a common objective: continually to reduce cost elements within the prices. Negotiations will then centre on the means and mutuality of achieving cost reductions (for example, improvements in quality performance, product design, manufacturing processes, scheduling, forecasting and so on).

Consider the following case study to highlight how communication with each other is needed.

CASE STUDY
TEXAS RANGERS

Pat Garrett and Billy the Kid were arrested by the Texas Rangers after a fight in the Laramie Saloon. They were strongly suspected of robbing the bank at Dead Man's Gulch, but the rangers had no proof. Pat and Billy were taken to separate jails and each was made the following offer knowing that the other was being offered the same:

- Option 1. If you confess to the armed robbery and your partner does not, we will speak up for you in court and you will only get one year in prison.
- Option 2. If you confess and your partner confesses, our plea for leniency will carry less weight and you will both get five years.
- Option 3. If you do not confess and your partner does not confess, you will both get two years for causing a disturbance of the peace.
- Option 4. If you do not confess but your partner does, you will bear the brunt of the punishment and get ten years.

The dilemma is clear. To protect themselves, each would confess, because no matter what the other one does, each will have done better for himself. However, this results in them both getting five years in prison, whereas by not confessing they would both get only two years and be better off. If they could have communicated with each other they might have agreed on a course of action that was better for both of them.

(*Source*: unknown)

Many companies are starting to view the buyer/seller relationship in the same light as shown in the above case study. They need to communicate fully with each other. Traditionally, the buyer's organisation has been responsible for making the final product and the supplier's organisation has been responsible for providing the components and materials.

Both functions have been seen as separate activities whereas of course they are interlinked. Communication between the two organisations has been guarded in case one can turn it to advantage, with possible adverse consequences for the other. The collaborative approach recognises that buyers' and sellers' organisations are interlinked by the reality of the supply chain that joins them.

The buyer recognises the fact that supplies are very much a part of the final product, and that working together with suppliers can increase the benefits to both parties.

PROBLEMS IN INTERCOMPANY RELATIONSHIPS

Whilst the benefits can be enormous, collaboration is not an easy practice to introduce successfully. There are many problems that have to be faced and overcome. Consider the following:

CASE STUDY
GENERAL MODEL OF NEGOTIATION – THE QUESTION

The 'Red Orange' bargaining game requires that individuals be paired into groups.

One person in each group plays the role of Dr Smith. He needs the juice from 2000 red oranges. Unless Dr Smith can obtain this juice, many lives will be lost to a rare disease, for which red orange juice is the cure.

Another person in each group plays the role of Dr Jones who needs the rinds from 2000 red oranges to cure another fatal disease.

Neither person in each group knows the other's role description.

Each person is also told that they have £250 000 to buy red oranges and that there are only 3000 red oranges available for sale from Mr Red (the game coordinator).

Dr Smith and Dr Jones are told either to agree on an offer to Mr Red or to submit competitive bids. If bidding is undertaken, it is 'winner takes all.'

A coin flip will determine the 'winner' if equal bids are submitted.

After five minutes of discussion, the two parties are to agree on a negotiation solution.

What do you think will happen?

The following are the options available:

1 Compete
If the parties submit competitive bids, one person will be totally successful; the other will be

---

a total failure. Competitive bidding arises as both parties typically do not communicate the juice versus rind issue to one another. Both parties think in terms of obtaining 2000 oranges and tend to treat each other as adversaries trying to obtain a scarce resource.

2 Collaborate

If the parties communicate and engage in joint problem solving, they may reach a collaborative solution in which one party uses the juice from 2000 oranges and the other party uses the rind from the same 2000 oranges. In this way, both parties can meet their objectives.

3 Compromise equally

If the parties fail to collaborate or compete, other techniques are possible. Each party may agree to share the loss and compromise by buying 1500 oranges apiece. Some sacrifice is required, but the parties will be making equal sacrifices and each party will be saving some lives.

4 Compromise unequally

Another possible solution occurs if one party accommodates the other. For example, if Dr Smith takes 1000 oranges and Dr Jones gets the remaining 2000 oranges, then Dr Jones reaches his goal because Dr Smith sacrifices his interest.

5 Walk out

Finally, both parties can conceivably walk out and fail to submit any resolution to Mr Red. This indicates total avoidance of the problem and results in the direst consequences – no cures are possible.

Conclusion

It will be seen that all of the non-collaborative options indicate some degree of failure, given the potential win-win solution to the exercise. In playing the game, non-collaborative solutions occur about 75 per cent of the time, usually because both parties approach the interaction with mutual suspicion.

Compete is most common, followed by compromising unequally.

(*Source*: unknown)

Buyer–seller relationships have been earlier defined on a scale that has adversarial/competing behaviour at one end and partnership/collaboration at the other. In Japan, relationships with suppliers tend towards the collaboration end of the scale, whilst in the UK the tendency is still towards the adversarial end. We do like to compete as 'We have been taught to compete; nobody has taught us to work together' (Alan Waller).

The following section on re-thinking tells us why this we do this and shows how we need to change.

Supply chain re-thinking

Many people do now understand what is involved when following a supply chain approach. However, ensuring the supply chain is optimised for the benefits of all participants will mean a re-thinking of traditional ways.

Such re-thinking may not be an easy process for some individuals in some companies and this may therefore limit the optimum development of supply chains. It would seem a possibility that supply chain development in the UK could fail because of the prevalent way of management thinking.

What, however, is sure, is that what worked for many years may not work for many more.

SUPPLY CHAIN DEVELOPMENT

Supply chains can be at various stages of development and the following gives a view of possible developments:

Stage	Structure of the supply chain	Some actions needed
Starting out	Fragmented and uncoordinated Low cost/service levels, high stock levels	Internal alignments Coordinate external suppliers Measure supply chain efficiency.
Getting there	Some working together but still high stock levels	Supply chain structure ICT systems internal/external for transparency/visibility
Arrived?	Has a supply chain structure but have slow growth and competition increasing	Develop new sales channels Modular products Direct delivery to customers Integrate fully the ICT systems
Re-birth	Static market growth	Increase outsourcing Strengthen existing relationships, branding, R&D, marketing
Starting out again	Virtual structures	Active monitoring and remain flexible for the next changes

CHANGES WHEN USING A SUPPLY CHAIN APPROACH

Taking a supply chain approach will require changes to the way things are done and the following briefly illustrates some of the needed changes:

Changes	Some of the needed 'ends' are:
'Silo' functions to 'holistic' processes	Decision integration, organisations of extended enterprises, collaborative management approaches, web connected, real-time focus, project management matrix structures
Product 'sells' to customer 'buys'	Demand pull, order driven, low to zero stock holding, involved suppliers, short production runs, real-time visibility, short product life cycles, fewer suppliers, market segmentation
Transactions to relationships	Dependency, commitment, cooperation, collaboration, aligned company cultures, extensive trust, proactive management

THE WAY WE LOOK

Taking a supply chain approach will require a business to change and this in turn will mean changing the thinking from a current and known position, towards a possibly unknown but planned-for future. As the way we think affects what we do, then the way we think is an important process to be considered.

Research suggests our brain is divided in two parts – the left hemisphere and the right hemisphere. At least, this is the simple view – front and back, and upper and lower quadrants are other divisions.

Meanwhile, the 'left and right' view suggests we have a logical left-side brain and a creative right-side brain. The left-side brain will firstly conduct an analysis, will then act, and finally will feel (for example, is the action 'correct' and 'right'). The right-side brain, however, works the other way: feeling, then action, then analysis.

Most people are relatively flexible in this brain wiring, and of course the influences of environmental forces and the way we are nurtured, treated, handled and so on also has a powerful impact on our thinking and on our personal behaviour. In exploring simply the left/right brain differences, the following differences are revealed:

Logical left-brain people	Creative right-brain people
Prefer written, mathematical, science-based approaches	Prefer musical, art/visual-based approaches
Objective, linear thinking, short-term views	Subjective, wholes/parallel processing, longer-term views
Analytical, step-by-step 'head' thinkers	Creative, free-flowing 'heart' thinkers
Rational facts-based reasoning that converges	Emotional 'feelings' synthesis that diverges
Summary: Analyses-acts-feels	Summary: Feels-acts-analyses

Most individuals can recognise which side is their personally representative one.

THE WAY COMPANIES MANAGE

As companies are collections of individuals, it is therefore possible to see left-sided and right-sided brain companies. Following on from the above individual brain-sided view, then companies may be viewed as follows:

Left-brain companies	Right-brain companies
Task based, 'today'	People based and a long-term view
Problems recur as only the symptoms are treated (sticking-plaster solutions)	Problems are tackled by looking at the thinking that causes the problems
Making/selling products/services has the priority	Make people before products/services
The way forward is with science/technology	The way forward is by motivating/empowering people
'The numbers speak for themselves'	'It is how we connect together that is important'
Incremental results/parts	Holistic, whole results/parts
More Western-culture based	More Eastern- and Latin-culture based

Left-brain companies will often work with fixed assumptions for development and growth as they are incapable of 'going outside of the box'. When they are pushed to change from tradition, they will react negatively as they fundamentally believe the way forward is 'more of the same'. They would see the only solution, for example to company growth, as needing a bigger share of the existing market.

SUPPLY CHAIN THINKING

These ways of thinking will also translate into company management approaches, including how supply chains are managed and structured, for 'as a person thinks then so they are' (Proverbs 23.7).

The following diagrams represent a hypothesis for the past and future of SCM.

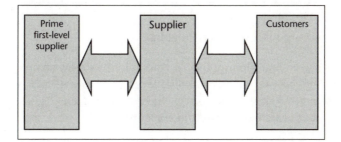

Figure 3.1   Older approach/linear thinking

The model in Figure 3.1 has given proven benefits, as will be shown later, to the previous non-supply chain ways of functional silo management.

It will be seen that this approach represents linear thinking, which is classically left-brain mode. This approach is also the major model currently used in the UK for supply chain development. By following the above left-brain explanations, we can see that this means having short-term task-centred approaches with an incremental view of the supply chain, with relationships to the next level only. This may or may not involve a collaborative approach and will more than likely have fixed arrangements and contracts in place. It will tend to use a rigid and reactive approach to customer service with scheduled and rational replenishment.

The supplier may also feel that the supply chain coordinations are all one way and that coercive power is being used; this being noted for example as 'the bullying and exploitation in which supermarkets indulge' (L. Michaels, March 2004).

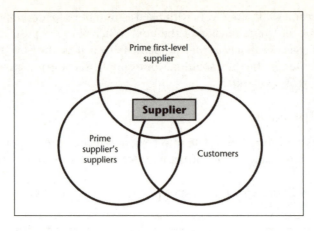

Figure 3.2   Newer approach/network thinking

Here (in Figure 3.2) is some attempt to go further into the supply chain using collaborative approaches and extend beyond the first supplier level. Fixed arrangements with boundaries/ contracts may exist but the collaboration will be more open and sharing. Customer service can be more responsive and flexible with real-time replenishments.

Figure 3.3   Emerging approaches/system thinking

In this seamless model shown in Figure 3.3, there are much more fluid arrangements, with systems thinking recognising the complex interactions that affect each other player in the specific supply chain. Right-brain thinking concentrates on the whole of the supply chain and uses seamless collaboration. Collaboration will be totally open and shared, and is unbound and innovative. Each specific supply chain could be viewed as a small company in itself comprising cross internal functions and jointly managed with suppliers/customers, perhaps following a matrix/project management structure organised into specific supply chain cells with decentralised control and shared responsibility from all involved. This follows the basic principles of 'small within big' that has, for example, worked successfully when adopting TQM and JIT methods for production cells internally within product manufacturing/assembly organisations. Interestingly, such approaches were pioneered in Japan, a more natural right-brain culture but of course have since been actively adopted and managed in the UK culture. Some changing in UK thinking therefore occurred!

A summary of the three models on supply chain thinking follows:

Old supply chain approach	Newer supply chain approach	Emerging supply chain approach
Linear thinking	Network thinking	Systems 'links and loops' thinking
Maybe collaborative at first level only	Collaborative and maybe beyond first levels	Collaborative and seamless in scope
Fixed contractual arrangements at 'arm's length'	Fixed arrangements/boundaries/ contracts	Virtual arrangements, unbounded and innovative
Horizontal flow chart shape	Venn shape	Petal/shamrock shape
'Rigid'	'Connected'	'Fluid'

CHANGING HOW WE THINK

Companies can be slow to change their thinking and there have been many well-known examples of former company sector leaders who have slipped from the number-one position and also examples of former state-owned monopoly companies that no longer exist.

In SCM, the consequence of 'sticking to the knitting' thinking can be as follows:

- adversary play-offs with suppliers;
- long production runs of unneeded products;
- 'just in case' expensive stock holding;
- customers get fed up and go elsewhere;
- inspection, reworking, warranty claims;
- vertical silo management structures;
- 'turf conscious' reactive 'fire-fighting' managers;
- 'rowing the boat' upstream and resisting change.

Companies are a collection of individuals and it is the thinking of the individuals in companies that needs to change. As has been noted above, individuals will tend to be more comfortable in one of the brain sides. This then means they can miss out on the other side. To be complete, we therefore need both sides. This is the classic whole-brain thinking. Clearly many companies do of course, try to reflect such whole-brain thinking through their recruitment policies and in the way they structure the organisation of the business.

But for efficient and effective SCM, companies and the individuals in companies need to take more conscious responsibility for the thinking. Business channels change and taking the view that supply chains now compete can mean thinking in a different way. Those individuals/companies who do not do this, may well find that they will not be invited to the party in the future. An example here is where a supply chain approach acknowledges that supplier numbers will be reduced; yet some suppliers will maintain a head-in-the-sand ostrich incremental approach, perhaps believing the reductions could not possibly affect them.

THINKING DIFFERENTLY

Each individual's brain is actually very similar to everyone else's, but the difference comes from how we use it. Individuals and companies should be challenged to use the brain differently.

If they are more creative right-brained, then the need is to be more logical left-brained. The following could be tried:

As individuals	For companies
Be on time for appointments	Keep promises and commitments
Practise and plan a step/step approach	Get the parts and processes working well, together
Time plan each step	Use time-based KPIs
Have a workspace that is ordered and structured	Reorganise the flows in the supply chain

If they are more logical left-brained, then the need is to be more creative right-brained. The following could be tried:

As individuals	For companies
Brainstorm to create ideas	Look at the whole supply chain beyond first-level suppliers
Make visual mind-map notes to enable free-flowing visual images	Make a supply chain map of the business and its supply chains
Explore a new neighbourhood	Explore how to get the people relationships 'right'
Try and understand your pet's feelings	Try to understand how the staff 'feel'

THE FUTURE: THE RIGHT- OR THE LEFT-BRAINED COMPANY?

The optimum and the whole will only of course be found by using both sides of the brain. A concern that remains with traditionally British left-brained thinking is that the trends and ways forward for SCM are never realised. This can mean for example missing a future of:

- long-term suppliers and joint action teams in the supply chain;
- short production runs with quick changeovers;
- minimal stockholding, JIT-type supply throughout the supply chain;
- being able to serve more demanding customers;
- obtaining right-first-time quality throughout the supply chain;
- having process and flatter cross-functional management structures;
- empowered proactive fire-lighting managers;
- continuous improvement and change.

Thinking right

To gain the benefits which collaboration has to offer, these differences in thinking need to be recognised. Choosing the best starting point is the key to a successful programme. Several companies have found from experience that actively educating and training suppliers produces more benefits than simply communicating a philosophy or new set of rules.

One company successfully introduced collaborative relationships in an entirely different way. Here a small group of suppliers was selected for a pilot scheme. The suppliers were chosen by two criteria:

- their relative importance to the company, for example turnover, parts count, technical criticality;
- the likelihood that they would be successful in a partnership relationship.

These criteria ensured a high level of confidence that the outcome would prove to be both successful and effective. The company was thus able to go through a learning curve with a small group of cooperative people.

This approach enabled the company to learn a lot about its own failing and to start to take action in-house. By the time they were ready to extend the scheme to more suppliers they already had a track record of improvement. This gave the company a base of credibility from which to start the process of persuasion with more suppliers.

THINKING WRONG

Unfortunately, relationships can have an adversarial side and these have already been examined and will also be examined further. Meanwhile, here are some suggestions for a resolution of the conflicts:

- *Authority.* The supplier is simply told by a buyer, who has the power, what the resolution will be. This method works against any collaborative approach because of the resentment that is generated within the supplier. There are also many situations where the buyer does not have absolute power to use such an authoritarian approach, as there are times when the supplier may have the advantage.

- *Single-sided trade-offs.* Here, companies make it possible for buyers and suppliers to live together although the conflict still exists. It is a means of maintaining the relationship even at the cost of poor solutions for both sides. Although it may often be necessary, it is not an ideal method for developing collaborative relationships. If reflects an inability to achieve agreement on the best of all possible solutions for both buyer and suppliers.

- *High-level/super goals.* Setting higher objectives than those generated by normal day-to-day operating conditions is a means of changing adversaries into partners. The threat of imported goods taking over a UK marketplace has caused many buyers and suppliers to work together instead of being adversaries and move towards collaborative relationships.

- *Open exchange.* Open exchange should be tackled slowly, starting with joint problem solving and gradually building as trust develops. Before embarking on this route, it is essential to map out the relative power structure as well as the relative strengths and weaknesses. This can be a high-risk method if it is not approached properly, but it forms the basis of any collaborative relationship.

Moving towards collaboration therefore involves changing attitudes, strategy and operating practices. There are no hard and fast rules for developing a programme because every purchasing organisation is different in its existing approach to its relationships with suppliers. Each needs to formulate its own plan of action based on its own operating environment. However, there is a set of broad guidelines that could be useful in developing partnership programmes. They address attitudes, strategy and operating practices.

ATTITUDE CHANGE AND PERSUASION

Suppliers are more likely to be convinced by buyers who:

* are considered to be reliable and have credibility;
* can demonstrate an understanding of the supplier's problems;
* recognise and can deal with the counter arguments.

As a first step within the organisation it is important to tackle the underlying factors that produce the level of competence and effectiveness that buyers need to pull the programme through.

Some suppliers will be more easily persuaded than others and the level of genuine commitment will vary. Suppliers will agree to collaborative relationships for many reasons:

* because the buyer has the power to reward – commitment will continue as long as the rewards are forthcoming;
* because there is prestige to be gained by being associated with the idea – this will last as the association remains important;
* because a supplier genuinely believes that collaborative relationships are the best way forward and will deliver benefits to them – this is the only permanent form of commitment.

Strategy changes

Change towards collaboration needs management to re-establish strategic aims. The following list includes some of the strategy issues that need to be examined with first-level suppliers to make them appropriate to a collaborative environment.

* The overall objective of the organisation may be to buy at the lowest available price. This needs to be expanded to take account of the lowest total cost of ownership to the company. Targets need to be set which include quality and delivery performance objectives and take account of the needs of the whole supply chain through to customer warranty and service considerations.

* Define the kind of suppliers who can best meet these objectives and then develop sourcing strategies for families of products. Suppliers need to have the capability to meet the quality and delivery performance criteria as well as make an active contribution towards reducing their own costs and pass on the benefits of lower prices.

- A gradual move towards long-term contracts with a single, but reliable source of supply gives suppliers security to implement investment and improvement programmes. In return they are able to commit to delivery and quality performance targets and year-on-year price reductions.

- Develop a material scheduling strategy that either gives the supplier stability or defines the percentage flexibility expected from the supplier. To do this, the purchasing operation may need to involve production as well as sales and marketing. Gaining commitment from within the organisation is often as challenging a task as gaining commitment from suppliers.

- Strategies for purchasing must take account of the technical requirements of the supplier base. Engineers and designers need to support the purchasing objectives and can make a key contribution to defining the technical aspects of a supplier's capability. Procurement must take account of engineers' or designers' needs in order to achieve the objective of lowest overall cost to the organisation.

Operating changes

Many of the operating procedures and practices will have grown up over the years from precedent or history. These need to be addressed and changed to support a collaborative relationship. Internal functions need to ensure that:

- Procedures and practice manuals or guidelines are revised to reflect changes in operating practice. This is often a good opportunity to rationalise and simplify procedure manuals that have become long and complex.
- The management and information reporting systems are changed to support the different priorities and objectives that are established.
- Buyers become familiar with the detail of their suppliers' processes; for example, suppliers have the opportunity to understand how their products fit into the buyer's manufacturing process.
- Specifications and quality acceptability requirements are clearly defined as or before the products are sent out on enquiry.
- Pre-release sourcing activities are introduced where cooperation between suppliers and the buying organisation on the design and development of bought in products can contribute to a better product.

Some organisations have introduced development agreements with suppliers that result from sourcing decisions taken well in advance of production releases or requisitions.

Sustaining strategic supplier collaboration

Collaboration will involve a management approach that seeks increased mutual buyer–supplier collaboration and trust, to improve productivity, quality and ultimately competitive advantage.

Specifically, a strategic collaboration is a relationship marked by mechanisms for buyer–supplier collaboration to solve problems and to share the benefits that are derived from quality or productivity gains that the joint efforts provide. Such collaboration is intended to provide competitive advantage to the buyer through greater flexibility, more technical input from the supplier, quicker response and reduced total procurement costs. The supplier gains through better planning information, greater demand security and, often, technical assistance from the buyer.

It is quite likely that such intercompany relationships will be dynamic, changing as they mature. Some claim that older collaborative relationships tend to develop wider involvement and better results, implying that, once established, most such relationships are destined not only to survive but to prosper. This may not be realistic. It may be more likely that some organisations manage their supplier relationships well, finding ways that increase the benefits to both themselves and their suppliers, whilst others find that the benefits eventually dwindle and do not warrant the higher cost of maintaining such relationships.

SUPPLIER COLLABORATION: FROM INITIATION TO MAINTENANCE

A variety of reasons have been cited to explain why organisations, particularly those in manufacturing, have formed longer-term, mutually beneficial supplier links or alliances. Such reasons are competitive pressure, a longer-term definition of cost, adoption of Japanese management methods, attempts to attain better supplier quality conformance or the adoption of JIT methods and so on.

Substituting a relationship for the traditional arm's-length transactional approach may increase the silo costs of procurement but could have wider trade-off returns that justify any added silo expenses. Japanese automakers for example have reduced both transaction costs and production costs. The former, because fewer, more concentrated suppliers require fewer resources to manage them and the production costs were reduced because of increases in scale economies and benefits from production smoothing.

These advantages may only be available from some supply chain relationships, as some supply chain combinations may not represent fertile ground for developing an alliance relationship. Research in several fields points to several prerequisites for the formation of supply chain alliances and partnerships. These are as follows:

- a match in the organisational and strategic objectives;
- a match in the values or philosophies regarding the management of the relationship;
- the availability of technical resources within the potential partner that could assist in solving problems;
- a willingness to provide planning and performance information;
- a belief by both parties that a collaborative approach would be mutually beneficial;
- the establishment of a measurement system to assess and share the benefits gained from the alliance/partnership in an equitable manner.

Conditions between organisations are likely to change over time. Good working relationships may build trust, leading in turn to expanded interaction. Alternatively, the relationship may falter as specific expectations are not met or one party finds diminishing returns from the effort to sustain the alliance's momentum. The critical factors for ensuring that the relationship is maintained may well not be those that necessarily were made when establishing the relationship in the first place.

DO RELATIONSHIPS TEND TO STRENGTHEN WITH TIME?

Relationships can often show improving results each year. This implies that the relationship stands to improve steadily as all involved, including the buyer and the supplier, interact more over time.

Relationships may last longer if the right elements are in place and both parties find it attractive to pursue greater involvement.

The authors' experience has shown a strong correlation between the strength of the relationship (as indicated by the amount of joint problem solving and benefit sharing arrangements between buyer and supplier), and the buyer's perception of its short-term and long-term benefits. Some relationships improved in their benefits over time more than others and it is likely to be those who functioned well at the start that would provide the most improvement.

WHY BOTHER?

Why then do some organisations choose to engage in the more difficult to manage and time-consuming pursuit of strategic supply chain relationships? Apart from the clear reason of the benefits that can be obtained, another reason is that the standards for supplier relations are gradually shifting, as the formation of supply chain relationships is becoming more of a prerequisite. For example, the need to lock in a technology supplier, reduce lead times or obtain assistance for component development may push organisations to enter into alliances with key suppliers. Rather than providing specific and distinct advantages, such moves may be simply to allow such organisations to maintain their competitive positions.

Maintaining such a relationship is likely to be more difficult to manage and also less likely to provide increasing benefits. Unlike managing pure legal and contractual-based transactions, supply chain relationships are likely to evolve and have different demands as they mature. As such relationships mature, the role of the buying organisation's purchasing philosophy becomes diminished in significance, while the amount and type of information shared by the supplier becomes the vital currency for building the stronger alliance relationships.

Dynamic requirements for building supply chain relationships

It is understandable that the critical inputs for relationship development may change as a relationship matures. It takes time for both parties to develop a common understanding of their respective roles. Further, trust is a key element in long-term relationships and takes time to develop and be tested.

Trust may be viewed as existing when one party has confidence in an exchange partner's reliability and integrity, or the expectation that the partner will behave predictably and not opportunistically. Trust will take some time and interaction to develop. It is a critical component and a prerequisite in collaborative relationships.

Conditions that promote the implementation of the supply chain relationship will then become less significant once the arrangements have become routine, while other factors will then arise in importance. Once the initial trust building phase is complete and the relationship has been set, other elements might come to the fore.

For strategic supply chain collaboration, commitments may increase through a movement towards single sourcing, with both buyer and supplier risking greater interdependence, or through expanded roles and responsibilities in delivering the alliance partner's products or services, with more intercompany exchange. For example in the early phases of relationship development, the buying company may initially be only expecting improved quality conformance, but as the alliance matures, then focus on improving design quality.

With increased interdependence over time, information exchange becomes a key element in relationship success (and failure). Information becomes the lifeblood of the relationship and also, the amount and type of information exchanged between buyers and suppliers may change as an alliance relationship matures.

We can divide the typical range of information passed between collaborative players into three categories:

- planning information;
- performance feedback;
- technological assistance.

Typically, most of the information would be expected to flow from buyer to supplier. While the initial information given to suppliers might centre on planning information, such as the buyer's production plans, the expectation is that the information will expand to include feedback about how well the supplier is meeting the buyer's needs and where areas for improvement lie.

Technological assistance may flow in either direction, with buyers sometimes providing supplier development expertise to improve the supplier's process and administrative practices and, less often, suppliers providing design expertise for the buyer's product or service designs. These types of information can be outlined in the order that they are likely to appear in maturing alliance relationships.

PLANNING INFORMATION

Often the first step in expanding the supply chain relationship is to provide the supplier with better information about likely demand. This information will usually be readily available and a means of sharing it with the supplier may be easily implemented. Giving the supplier longer-term estimates of volume and order timing allows them to plan better, avoid short-term rush jobs and their consequent quality problems, and to better utilise capacity. The results can be lower costs and fewer missed deliveries.

Supply chain collaboration should allow both parties to benefit from the improvements, with the buyer getting a more predictable source and the supplier reducing costs and risks.

PERFORMANCE FEEDBACK

Many organisations establish evaluation and feedback systems, aimed at a supplier's delivery performance and product/service quality. An annual evaluation is not only used to help suppliers target areas needing improvement but also is factored into the assessment of the supplier's bid price for future contracts.

If the information flow is a critical requirement for the development of the supply chain collaboration, then the feedback mechanism's characteristics will have a strong bearing on how well the relationship flourishes.

Therefore, there are two elements to consider:

- process – such as electronic data exchange versus personal contact, frequency of data exchange and the degree of confidence placed in the source of the feedback;
- content – such as the information's timeliness, relevancy and completeness.

Clearly, the information process structure, the type of problem and the degree of difference between the organisations will seriously impact how the supplier perceives the information's value.

TECHNOLOGICAL ASSISTANCE

A distinguishing feature of supply chain collaboration is the flow of technology between buyer and supplier. For smaller supplier organisations, the technology flowing from the buyer is often the expertise in designing production and delivery systems. In turn, the buyer may seek the supplier's help when designing the components to be sourced.

The promise of gaining technology from the supply chain collaboration can often be a major reason for its formation. Arguably, the flow of technology represents more commitment to an intercompany relationship than the other forms of information and more trust may need to be developed before there is the anticipated flow of technology. However, the failure to realise the anticipated or expected technological benefits can sour the relationship. Thus, the gap between expected and delivered technological benefits over time is likely to have a significant impact on the ultimate success of the alliance. Further, more than any other component of the information exchange relationship, technology flows are anticipated in both directions (for example, from buyer to supplier and from supplier to buyer).

INFORMATION: VITAL TO SUCCESS

These types of information are vital determinants of long-term alliance success. As with marriages, communication helps to establish expectations, air points of dissatisfaction and provide needed support and assistance. The willingness to share important information is a primary basis for trust, without which the alliance is not likely to succeed.

Moreover, the collaborative players may have rising expectations about the type of information that is forthcoming from their counterparts. Planning information alone may be satisfactory in the initial stages of alliance development, while performance feedback may mark increased commitment from the buyer organisation to create added administrative systems to improve the supplier's capabilities. Technological assistance may not be forthcoming until commitment and trust is more fully developed. The alliance's success is likely to be affected by how well these forms of information are forthcoming compared to each partner's expectations.

CASE STUDY
BENEFITS OF IMPROVED RELATIONSHIPS

Three-quarters of UK companies believe collaborative supply chain partnerships are either important or very important to their business goals.

Research commissioned by BT and conducted by analysts IDC, found that of the companies that measured the impact of partnerships, over 60 per cent of small- and medium-sized enterprises said close relationships increased revenues.

Half of the large organisations had increased profits. The biggest benefit for all respondents was increased efficiency, especially for large companies. The research also found that according to more than 60 per cent of respondents, a shared vision by all participants is the attribute most likely to lead to a successful partnership arrangement.

'A vision is absolutely essential,' said Les Pyle, director-general of Partnership Sourcing Ltd (PSL), a non-profit organisation set up by the Confederation of British Industry and the Department of Trade and Industry in 1990 to help foster strategic long-term supply chain relationships.

Pyle stressed that well-intentioned mission statements are not visions and are unlikely to lead to successful collaboration. 'A partnership must be kept under review and include measurable goals, such as market share,' he said. 'The more you can measure efforts, the more likely you will be successful.'

Although most companies in the survey claimed benefits from partnerships, 68 per cent had not attempted to measure the financial impact and 58 per cent said they had no plans to measure it. The research covered 250 companies and was conducted in January and February 2004.

The following diagram illustrates the full research results for both small and large organisations in the private sector.

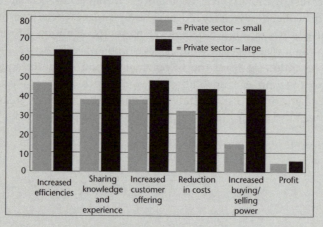

Figure 3.4   The objective of collaborative projects

(Research: BT)

CASE STUDY

BENEFITS OF IMPROVED RELATIONSHIPS – FASSON/WORSLEYS

The partnership between brush supplier Fasson in Holland and automotive testing company Worsleys in the UK, clearly demonstrates that if both companies are committed to it, a close and trusting relationship really can work well, and quickly result in outstanding bottom-line benefits.

How does this work?
What circumstances led to this partnership and how have Fasson and Worsleys profited from this arrangement?

Fasson initiated a project to establish partnerships with their existing customers in a vendor-managed inventory (VMI) and zero-cost transaction programme. Their aim was to improve performance and results in six key areas:

- purchasing
- planning
- warehousing
- inventory holding
- administration
- finance.

Alongside these they wanted to increase the use of automatic transactions using EDI facilities with the eventual goal of supplying customers with their products without using any administrative systems or support thus rendering them 'zero cost'.

Advanced skills
Customer Worsleys and supplier Fasson had a long-standing business relationship and as one of its largest UK customers it was natural for Fasson to approach Worsleys when it decided to instigate a partnership programme. When Fasson approached Worsleys they were as much interested in the software they had implemented to improve sales forecasting and stock control as they were in the VMI plans. After long and detailed discussions, however, they realised that their business objectives matched exactly those of Fasson: to improve inventory performance and service levels whilst simultaneously reducing transaction costs.
An initial agreement was put in place, with the following features:

- a modem link was installed for Fasson to dial into Worsleys;
- agreed stock level parameters were established;
- a file was set up which collected all the necessary information about Worsleys daily sales forecast and order planning;
- Worsleys input 42 months' sales history data for forecasting purposes;
- a daily file including all on-hand balances, customer orders and scheduled receipts was set up for Fasson to access.

Both companies were totally committed from day one and they agreed to trust each other and the system. Not many people take the risk, which is why so many businesses pay mere lip service to partnerships. Of course they tracked the performance, but they had confidence in the parameters they had agreed and the faith not to tamper with them if results were not instantly what were expected. In fact in the year in which it has been operating, they have made only a few minor adjustments to fine-tune it.

Impressive results

At Worsleys, inventory value has been reduced by £1 million in one year. Customer service has increased from what was an already high 90 per cent to 99 per cent, and this is in a business where same-day deliveries are the normal expectation. Paperwork has reduced significantly and deliveries from Fasson are more regular and more smoothly dealt with.

They are delighted with the benefits of the partnership, but there is much more they can achieve. EDI communications have now replaced the modem facility and they are planning to implement automatic invoicing and payment, which will further reduce transaction costs. The effect on stock has been dramatic, but hand in hand with the reduction has been an increase in the range of products, which means an improvement in customer service and sales.

Inventory levels

The major benefits have been in inventory levels. They no longer have to forecast sales as they have the facts on line. This in turn means smooth production plans. The reduction in transaction costs realises more profit for Fasson without price increases to the customer. Now that they have proven the worth of the partnership with Worsleys, they are expanding into other customers.

Benefits of better relationships

The following are some of benefits of collaboration in the supply chain that are possible:

Aspect	Collaboration brings
Forecast accuracy	Increased external visibility will force better accuracy
Lead time	Reductions following sharing and joint improvements
Inventory	Reduced as stock levels fall
Utilisation of resources	Improved in a leaner operation with less waste
Costs	Reduced and improved
Service levels	Increased and improved
People	Trust and improved relationships

To summarise the benefits from taking a collaborative SCM approach:

Doing something What needs to be done	Doing nothing What happens when nothing is done
A few long-term suppliers and joint action teams	Adversary, play-offs with suppliers
Short production runs with quick changeovers	Long product runs of products no longer needed
Minimal just-in-time stockholding	Expensive just-in-case stockholding
Customers who are more demanding	Customers who get fed up, so go elsewhere
Right-first-time quality throughout	Inspections, reworking, warranty claims
Process and flatter cross-functional management structures	Vertical, silo management structures
Empowered, proactive fire-lighting managers	Turf-conscious, reactive fire-fighting managers
Continuous improvement and change	Rowing the same boat but against the current, and resisting change

4 *Changing and Improving Supply Chain Relationships*

The secret ingredient lies in the relationships amongst all parts.

Johnson and Broms: *Profit Beyond Measure: Extraordinary
Results through Attention to Work and People* (2000)

In Part 4, we examine how to maintain collaborative relationships and the right environment. The stages in development of relationships are explored. This means looking at the expectations of buyers and sellers, mutual understanding, and performance monitoring and corrective actions.

Relationships and trust are next looked at, along with what needs to be done to build trust, including at strategic levels.

Changing relationships can bring implementation problems, and we review case studies, including the pitfall and success factors. There is no one size fits all implementation, as a mix/match approach is often needed. The use of case studies therefore provides a useful 'toolkit' for readers to dip into and use as appropriate.

Implementation involves change; this is never easy and the key aspects involved in change are therefore looked at. This includes examining people's reactions and resistance, the dynamics of change and its effect on people's behaviour.

We provide a vision for the relationship-driven supply chain with our views of the world-class supply chain and the eight supply chain rules. Next we look at the relationship between thinking, structure and managing.

Finally, we provide a model for supply development and change.

Maintaining collaborative buyer–supplier relationships

Collaborative relationships permit companies to strengthen their competitive positions by concentrating joint efforts on improving areas of mutual concern, such as quality, productivity delivery and customer satisfaction.

The cumulative success of such initiatives is normally the result of mutual efforts that are focused on:

- improved communication;
- clarification of needs and expectations;
- elimination of problems and concerns;
- consistent performance;
- creation of competitive advantages.

Effective supply chain collaboration is also instrumental in stimulating cross-functional activity within the individual companies, resulting in cross-functional improvements and improved communication between companies.

WHAT RESEARCH HAS DISCOVERED

The importance of communication flow and the sharing of information for effective collaboration are borne out by the following McKinsey research into collaboration.

CASE STUDY
COLLABORATION – NECESSARY BUT DIFFICULT

Eighty-four per cent of executives at companies with annual revenues exceeding $30 billion stressed the importance of collaboration, both internally and across business units externally.

One significant problem appears to be that executives cannot obtain the information that they need to make effective decisions. For instance, 40 per cent said that their companies do not share distinctive knowledge across business units effectively, and 39 per cent stated that they have difficulty finding the correct knowledge needed to make company-wide decisions.

Other key roadblocks also impede effective collaboration. A key problem is that different business units tend to have different structures, such as varying definitions of roles and functions that are actually quite similar. Overall, more than three-quarters of executives stated that this problem complicates collaborative efforts. Furthermore, nearly 60 per cent of all executives stated that they do not measure collaboration effectively. If this is the case, it is of no surprise that there is still a long journey for many companies before they can enjoy the benefits of collaboration that we are advocating in this book.

Finally, since the collaboration needed to build intangible assets such as strong customer–supplier relationships can demand an open-ended time commitment; a strong focus on quarterly results and yearly outcomes may also be a problem. Nearly two-thirds of the sample researched say that their companies focus on short-term results to the detriment of longer-term results which could be more substantial through greater long-term collaboration.

(*Source*: *2005 Survey of Global Business Executives*, McKinsey Quarterly)

A number of other researchers have written about how to develop and manage buyer–supplier relationships. The major findings of their studies are summarised below:

- Buyer–supplier collaborative relationships can offer positive and clear-cut advantages to both parties.
- Guidelines for deciding when to use collaboration and how to select partners can be developed.
- Specific guidelines for establishing buyer–supplier collaboration can be developed.
- Buyer–supplier collaboration creates an important path for the developing of total quality in the organisation.
- A strategic view suggests that successful collaboration must include defining collaboration types and management modes, coupled with the mapping of potential relationships.

However, only a limited amount of research has examined the factors behind the survival and progression of collaborative buyer–supplier relationships. Key findings here are as follows:

- Product information and social exchange among partners lead to both cooperation and adaptation. Adaptation is the process of making investments in the relationship, and is affected by the degree of coordination and cross-functionality between the organisations,
- The maintenance of long-term relationships requires an ongoing commitment from both parties if they are to continually improve.
- Partners must develop trust and assure commitment through open and candid communication, shared product and process developments, achievement of joint performance requirements and positive responses to performance problems.

Trust and commitment clearly are a result of all players' behaviour. The degree of trust and commitment between a buyer and a supplier in partnership can be threatened, however, when one of them is placed in an uneconomical position. For example, a seller may delay deliveries when it can sell its products on the spot market in excess of the stipulated contract price, or a buyer may rely on the spot market to obtain lower prices than those specified in an agreement. Similarly, under financial distress, both may postpone or suspend expenditures by delaying or foregoing certain commitments.

Therefore, collaborative relationships have an implicit feature of possible performance problems, which can be detrimental if they affect mutual expectations underpinning the commitments of the partners. Thus, a mechanism should be in place to handle these deviations.

The source of problems in collaborative relationships can often be traced to the environment, as shown in Figure 4.1.

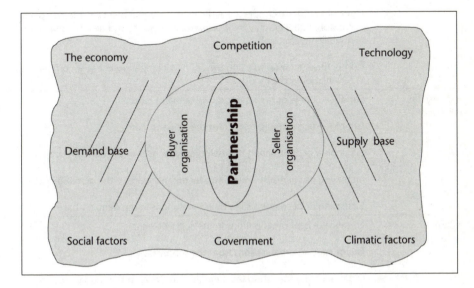

Figure 4.1   Buyer–supplier collaborative environment

Changes in any environment component can affect the expectations or perceptions of performance. They require adjustment by the buyer, the seller or both, to maintain a viable relationship.

The environment is made up of a number of factors:

- external elements – economic, climatic, social, technological, government, competition;
- demand base;
- supply base;
- buying organisation;
- selling organisation;
- the partnership itself.

Specific changes that may occur and require adaptation to maintain the relationship are highlighted below:

Components of the buyer–supplier relationship environment

External	The economy (for example recession, recovery, prosperous business cycle, inflationary or deflationary trends; monetary policies, interest rates, fiscal policies, tax rates, balance of payment, surpluses, deficits)
	Climatic factors (for example weather changes, natural disasters, environment issues)
	Social factors (for example personal values and attitude shifts)
	Technology (for example new product or process advancements)
	Government (for example domestic content requirements, wage and price controls, equal employment opportunities, safety and health regulations, disability legislation)
	Competitive (for example entrance of new competition or new competitive advantages in the industry)
Demand base for supplier	Entrance of new organisations in the demand base
	Exit of existing organisations from the demand base
	Expanding or contracting technological advances in the demand base
	Increasing or decreasing purchases by organisations in the demand base
	Increasing or decreasing sales by organisations in the demand base
Supply base for buyer	Entrance of new organisations in the supply base
	Exit of existing organisations from the supply base
	Expanding or contracting technological advances in the supply base
	Increasing or decreasing purchases made by organisations in the supply base
	Increasing or decreasing sales by organisations in the supply base

Buyer and seller	Strategic intent (for example acquiring new technologies to exploit future opportunities, opening new markets, capturing existing markets, exploiting competitors' weaknesses, expanding into global markets)
	Strategic match (for example implementing TQM concepts, embracing JIT philosophies, requiring continual improvement objectives, installing cycle time reduction goals)
	Change of ownership (for example acquisition of one of the partners by a third party, having unequal share of financial responsibility in the partnership)
Relationship	Performance problems (for example quality performance problems, late or missed deliveries, withholding or delaying necessary information)
	Change of key personnel (for example reassignment of partnership champion, assignment of new employees to partnership team)
	Organisational socialisation (for example establishing the partnership team's importance, purpose and identity, setting team tasks, enriching team potency, training existing and new members, setting up relationships amongst members)

Stages in the development of a collaborative relationship

Managers have described successful buyer–seller relationships in terms of fulfilling the mutual expectations. Unsuccessful collaborative relationships have been described in terms of not meeting the expectations held by one or both partners. Of course, other factors may also affect the ability of a collaborative relationship to succeed.

A primary factor in the development and maintenance of sound buyer–seller collaborative relationships is the partners' expectations and perceptions of each other's performance. When expectations are not fulfilled, or there is a misinterpretation of expectations, a collaborative relationship will experience an unexpected shock in its operating system.

An approach to developing and maintaining collaborative relationships is therefore detailed below in five stages:

- Stage 1: Buyer's expectations
- Stage 2: Seller's perceptions
- Stage 3: Mutual understanding and commitment
- Stage 4: Performance activity
- Stage 5: Corrective action.

During the performance stage the relationship may experience departures from expectations established when the collaborative relationship was developed, thus typically reducing the stability of the relationship. The relationship then moves to Stage 5, corrective action, where alternatives are available to mitigate the performance disruption and bring stability back to the collaborative relationships. This is shown diagrammatically in Figure 4.2.

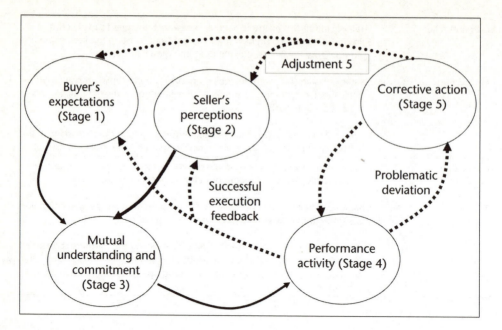

Figure 4.2 Buyer–supplier collaborative relationship model

STAGE 1: BUYER'S EXPECTATIONS

A primary reason for buying organisations to develop collaborative relationships with suppliers is to become more competitive. A competitive advantage can be enhanced by contributions from suppliers in areas such as quality, cost, delivery, product development, product and process innovations and productivity. Through collaborative relationships, buyers induce selected suppliers to become contributors to the buying organisation's competitive posture.

Instead of diversifying risk by spreading purchases over a number of suppliers and switching from one supplier to another to obtain desirable performance, a collaborative relationship concentrates efforts with one supplier to continuously improve performance in critical areas.

For a seller to become a contributor to a buying organisation's competitive posture, it is imperative that buyers consciously formulate and develop expectations of performance and contributions the partner will make to the buying organisation's competitive position. Precise expectations define the type of working relationships a buyer desires from its supply player and determine the degree of commitment required to achieve the desired results.

Unless these expectations are clearly communicated to a prospective player, a great potential exists for misperceptions by either party. If left unchecked, this could lead to problematic deviations within a collaborative relationship after it is established.

Once potential players' performance expectations have been formulated and understood, they should be translated into specific selection and subsequent performance criteria.

Most collaborative relationships, however, require a careful assessment of things, such as the organisation's basic management philosophy and managerial attitudes toward quality, collaborative problem solving and so on, because these less tangible factors often can be more important than specific operational criteria. In such cases, a buyer may have performance expectations requiring the potential supplier to have:

- strong top management commitment;
- desire to work toward continuous improvement;
- focus on elimination of production process variation;
- desire for open and candid communication;
- knowledge of the buyer's business, products and their applications;
- the capability to deliver within time and cost constraints.

In other words, buyers must know their needs and expectations before developing a collaborative relationship arrangement, and these must be communicated unambiguously to the potential partner.

STAGE 2: SELLER'S PERCEPTION

A seller's perception and knowledge of its targeted customers' needs should drive its operational and strategic decisions. Additionally, a clear perception of a specific buyer's needs and expectations facilitates a seller's response to a proposal request.

The more accurately the seller understands the buyer's expectations, the more likely it is that the proposal will match the actual requirements of the buyer. However, in today's business environment of shifting priorities, numerous false starts and conflicting communications, sellers often lose sight of a buyer's expectations. Suppliers may not always understand what types of activities and levels of performance are necessary to match or exceed a buyer's expectations. This lack of understanding can have a detrimental effect on the proposal developed, negotiations conducted and the performance executed by the seller during the critical period of relationship development.

The seller's perceptions of a buyer's expectations are partially based on communications, history or experience, and the buying organisation's credibility. For example, a buyer may say that quality and delivery are primary requirements, yet decisions may appear to be based largely on price. The more a purchaser communicates its needs and expectations and the more consistently it executes its intentions and requirements, the clearer the seller's perceptions of the purchaser become, thus facilitating a strategic match of the two.

STAGE 3: MUTUAL UNDERSTANDING AND COMMITMENT

Awareness and detailed knowledge of each partner's requirements and expectations are necessary to achieve a mutual understanding of performance requirements for collaborative relationships. This essential background information is obtained through an exchange of information about the partners' technical abilities, operational capabilities and managerial philosophies.

The partners must express a genuine commitment to the relationship and a corresponding desire to work toward its continuous improvement. It is on this foundation that partners can begin to reconcile differing expectations, establish measurements and use corrective action plans to eliminate waste, and move to a higher level of competitive advantage. Without this mutual exchange of information, the partners are destined to operate in a system with:

- conflicting measurements;
- inappropriate definitions of customer service;
- inaccurate performance status;
- ineffective information systems;

- discrimination against certain customers;
- poor coordination;
- inappropriate shipping methods;
- organisational barriers.

Within the context of a collaborative relationship, the exchange of information must occur between those individuals who will be involved in the relationship.

Open and candid communication flow at all levels and across functional areas of the two organisations is essential for successful collaborative relationships development. Negotiations must give way to dialogue if collaborative relationships are to be successful: relationships are held together by the sharing of information.

To perform effectively, each participating individual must have a precise understanding of his or her specific role in the relationship and must understand how it contributes to the success of the collaborative relationship – ultimately adding value for the final customers.

STAGE 4: PERFORMANCE ACTIVITY

During this culminating stage of the collaborative relationships, the roles of each participant usually become firmer and clearer. As each organisation successfully fulfils its responsibilities, the original expectations are usually reinforced, leading to the development of satisfaction and mutual trust. Successful fulfilment of the relationship's performance requirements is shown as performance feedback to the buyer's expectations (Stage 1) and the seller's perception (Stage 2).

However, failure adequately to discharge one's responsibilities can create a performance deviation that may result in dissatisfaction and if left unresolved might threaten the viability of the partnership. When such a deviation occurs, the approach shows performance feedback going to Stage 5, corrective action. In this stage, the deviation is addressed with the objective of stabilizing the performance activity. Consequently, it is essential that each of the players' participating personnel know specifically what is expected and what they can expect from their counterparts.

Even though a collaborative relationship is effectively providing mutual benefits to the players, all buyer–supplier relationships are subject to possible performance problems that can be detrimental to either or both of the two organisations. Correspondingly, a corrective action stage is necessary to mitigate performance problems.

STAGE 5: CORRECTIVE ACTION STAGE

When a variation from expected performance occurs, the stability in Stage 4 of the relationship can be lost and that may jeopardise the viability of the collaborative relationships. Such variations often result from ambiguous responsibilities or unanticipated events in the relationship environment. At this point, the contribution of the relationship to one or both of the participants may be questionable, and in turn may threaten the mutual commitment and trust essential to effective operation of the relationship.

Partners can respond to performance variations by taking corrective action in the following three distinct ways:

Operational unilateral adjustment

Here, the individuals causing the variation make necessary unilateral adjustments to re-establish performance stability, once the cause of the variation is recognised.

Operational bilateral adjustment

This requires joint efforts by both parties in identifying and eliminated the variation, again with the object of restoring performance stability.

Managerial bilateral adjustment

The variation is brought to the attention of senior managers of both participants, where the expectations and performance requirements of each participant can be clarified or renegotiated to reinstate performance stability. If the causes of the problem cannot be resolved by mutual agreement, or if the partners' senior managers cannot alter expectations, then they should seriously consider terminating the partnership.

MANAGERIAL IMPLICATIONS IN THE FIVE STAGES

As buying and selling organisations contemplate the use of collaborative relationships to achieve mutual benefits, they must be aware that both organisations need to develop a commitment to each other. However, even the best-negotiated and agreed-upon relationships typically are subject to some unforeseen events or variation in expected performance.

If the players cannot readjust or renegotiate (externally or internally) their expectations to restore performance stability and re-establish their commitment to each other, the relationships should be terminated.

Meanwhile, the following implications seem to be potentially instructive for senior managers who are contemplating or are involved in a buyer–seller partnership:

Checklist: Best practice in supply chain collaboration

*   Promote cooperation and trust among all those involved in buyer–seller partnerships.
*   Encourage open communication among personnel at both organisations participating in a buyer–supplier partnerships.
*   Advocate the competitive advantages available to both organisations participating in buyer–supplier partnerships.
*   Sanction the need for mutual benefits to both organisations taking part in buyer–supplier partnerships.
*   Support the expectations underpinning buyer–supplier partnerships.

Additionally, the following implications seem to be potentially instructive for managerial and operating personnel involved in a buyer–supplier partnership.

*   Meet the performance requirements consistently, according to the expectations of the buyer–supplier partnership agreements.

- Acknowledge and resolve quickly any deviations to the expected partnership performance.

Relationships and trust

Trust will often remain a major barrier and without trust, there will be no relationship. Trust is fundamentally about having to give up to another what you personally believe is valuable to you, it is 'One for all and all for one' and it is a willing interdependence. Trust is built when behaviour matches expectations and involves consistency in motives and accountability for actions. Trust becomes a self-fulfilling prophecy.

Trust is firstly built between people, one on one, and is not something that is built remotely, between nebulous companies. Trust between companies will only follow on from the trust of individuals inside those companies.

Fortunately trust can be won by consistently telling the truth in a way that others can verify. Trust in this way is about transparency and includes the admission of mistakes and not covering them up. Building trust 'one on one' involves the following:

- doing what you say you will do;
- going beyond conventional expectations;
- undertaking open and honest communication;
- being patient;
- accepting and admitting to mistakes;
- ensuring the other party gets a fair outcome.

Trust defies logic. Some people trust straight away with no real basis (a good thing, as this is the basis for society and community). Some people will need to see repeated behaviour before they will trust. Some will need consistency in behaviour for months or years. Some will never trust.

Trust however has a critical and sound logic aspect: trust reduces uncertainty; there is no second guessing, what they say is true; commitments are honoured and therefore bargaining, monitoring and handling disputes are all minimised.

Trust and collaboration are partners. Collaboration requires trust when sharing together and involves:

- shared goals = common purpose, collective commitment, agreeing the business we are in;
- shared culture = agreed values that bind us together, working cooperatively to the common goal;
- shared learning = pooling talent, skills, knowledge, reflecting, reviewing, revising and changing together;
- shared effort = one approach with flexible teams;
- shared information: the right information is shared with the right people for the right reasons, where the:
  - right information = that which is used to give better service and reduce costs;
  - right people = are those who can use it to help you;
- right reasons = that which will reduce, save, improve, quicken and so on.
  (Source: after *Partnerships with People,* DTI)

Collaboration is working together jointly and to be effective requires trust. It is a powerful strategy that will need to start internally (win the home games first), and then extend externally into those specific supply chain networks that have been identified that will benefit from such a relationship-driven approach. Incompatible attitudes, values and beliefs about trust and collaboration between the supply chain players can only lead to lost opportunities.

The following series of checklists provide overviews of this critical component.

Checklist: Trust is/is not

Trust is	Trust is not
Confidence in own and others' abilities	Blind faith in the unknown
Experienced by working together with integrity, honesty and openness	Cheap, as there is high cost of failure. Sometimes failure is critical
A positive power using both the heart and the head	A single 'my' view
Learning and being flexible and willing to change	Formal rules
Tough and confronting without bring confrontational, as expectations have to be met	Easy
Bonding, intimacy and working together face to face	Keeping your distance
Leadership is visible and driven by vision and clear missions that create the right atmosphere of trust	Invisible leadership
A genuine belief system that sees it is the right thing to do as all will benefit	Used temporarily or short term or for single benefit

Checklist: Levels of trust

Level one	Level two	Level three
Boundary trust	Reliable trust	Goodwill trust
Contractual	Competence	Commitment
Explicit promises	Known standards	Anything that is required to foster the relationship
Standard performance	Satisfactory performance	Success beyond expectation
Mistakes bring enforcement		Mistakes give shared learning for advantage
Exchange data for transactions	Cooperate on information for mutual access	Cognitive connections and joint decision making
Animal brain		Human brain
Symbonic	Share	Swap
Time bound (as far as the contract says)		Open ended, ongoing and leaving a legacy

Checklist: Building trust

Show acceptance	Be non-judgemental of others: value diversity Appreciate people: critique tasks, processes and systems React to data, not rumour
Be open	Initiate self-disclosure; reveal your thinking and feelings Volunteer information Reveal your values and priorities
Be congruent and honest	Say what you think; state your opinion, even when different from others State your wants and needs Encourage honesty in others State clearly what you will and will not reveal
Be reliable:	Do what you say you will do; see that your organisation does what you say it will do Set clear and realistic limits on both sides Treat commitments seriously and develop reliable processes Influence your own organisation to remove win/lose practices
Strive for continuous improvement	Understand and measure the processes that most affect the relationship Continuously improve processes and behaviours (a goal of any healthy relationship) Investigate opportunities for more benefit for the relationship Influence your organisation to create more mutual benefit for the relationships Exchange candid feedback on how well the relationship is working
And finally	All parties must come to believe that the others will do what they have said they will do All parties must find a way to be comfortable with the risk of being open and vulnerable to the others, in the secure belief that the other parties will not take unfair advantage All must show willingness to help the others become more successful Broken agreements destroy trust and lead to bad implementations and performance Continuous improvement is the fabric and product of trust in a relationship

Strategic trust in supply chain collaboration

One of the key distinguishing characteristics of a high-performance supply chain collaborative relationship is the presence of strategic trust. With strategic trust, the parties have access to each other's strategic plans in the pertinent areas of the interface. Relevant cost information and forecasts are shared. Risks and rewards are addressed openly.

Some may believe trust can only exist between individuals. However, trust must also be institutionalised at the intercompany level if organisations are to enjoy the full benefits of improved supply chain relationships. Trust must be a part of the company culture and therefore, become 'the way we do things around here'.

Buyer–supplier trust: Prerequisites

Satisfaction with the relationship	Both sides must feel that they can gain from the relationship
Shared long-term objectives	The parties to a preferred supply chain relationship must share long-term objectives for their areas of internal dependency
Respect for each other's rights, needs and opinions	Parties to a preferred supply chain relationship are equals. Discussions are conducted in an atmosphere of respect and long-term advantage
Flexibility of relationship	Preferred supply chain relationships are adaptable in their focus
Empathy for the other party	Both parties work at understanding issues that arise from the other party's point of view
Cultural compatibility	Potential parties to a preferred supply chain relationship must examine each other's culture to maximise the probability of a good fit or at least to ensure a thorough understanding of unavoidable differences
Atmosphere of cooperation	An atmosphere of cooperation must be established, maintained and nurtured
Acknowledged interdependence	All players from both organisations must recognise that 'we need them as much as they need us'
Top management involvement	Preferred supply chain relationships require active top management involvement
Tight operating linkages	Communication must be planned for and facilitated
Openness in technical areas of cooperation	Forecasts, production plans, technology advantages must be shared by the parties to a preferred supply relationship
Open books on common projects	Cost data relevant to the project must be shared
Application knowledge	Application knowledge must be planned for and managed
Managers responsible for the relationship	The parties to a preferred supply chain relationship must appoint and support supply account managers within both organisations
Conflict	Disagreements will arise in almost any relationship, how they are resolved is crucial
Team development training	Members of all cross-functional teams (customer, supplier, intercompany) receive team development training
Intercompany team relations	Intercompany team members maintain a constructive, problem-solving attitude with their team mates
Ethics	Involved personnel of both organisations operate ethically and trust their counterparts ethically
Negotiations	Negotiations are conducted in a manner designed to develop and reinforce trust
Training in the development of strategic alliances	Personnel from both organisations involved in the development of strategic alliances receive guidance, training and/or experience in prerequisite skills
Specific trust building activities	Personnel at both organisations take specific planned actions designed to develop trust
Cross-functional team selection	Members of your, your counterpart's and the intercompany cross-functional teams are selected very carefully for both technical expertise and behavioural skills
Organisational style	Cross-functional teams should be a way of life at both organisations

Changing organisational behaviour

When making fundamental changes to supply chain relationships, there is the knock-on effect of having to change organisational behaviour patterns. This cannot be avoided. Buying behaviour and supplier relationships will be directly involved in changing and shifting.

SHIFT IN ORGANISATIONAL BUYING BEHAVIOUR

Customers realise that suppliers create value and that those suppliers who provide access to value creation will provide them with sustainable competitive advantages. Value creation can manifest itself into access to technology, access to markets and access to information.

Commitment and trust on the part of the supplier has to be acknowledged as being critical by buyers. However, the aspects of trust and commitment from the buyer's perspective will not be easy as buyers have traditionally been quite willing to regularly change suppliers.

Customers may not like to reduce their supplier choices however because of the fear that they will be dependent on a smaller set of suppliers. This results in the lack of a trusting relationship. Most suppliers, therefore in turn, do not trust their customers. This is changing: for example, Xerox reduced the number of suppliers and found that they obtained better services and prices. The reduction in suppliers is a common and widespread trend when a choice is made to work differently in supplier relationships.

RELATIONSHIP WITH SUPPLIERS: THE NEXT FRONTIER

There are four underlying reasons for improving supplier relationships. These are:

- increased cost efficiency;
- increased effectiveness;
- enabling technologies;
- increased competitiveness.

Improved supplier relationships will reduce some of the costs associated with order transactions. In situations of multiple suppliers, both buyers and suppliers feel a high level of uncertainty and therefore there are multiple controls to ensure successful transactions. Control increases costs and decreases the efficiency of the relationship. In contrast, supplier relationships reduce uncertainty with increased efficiency of transactions.

Because of better information technology, organisations can track the actual cost of every transaction. Suppliers will be able to determine that it is not cost effective to provide their services to all of their customers. This will lead to a decrease in the number of customers for suppliers.

Supplier relationships can also enhance the effectiveness of organisations. Organisations may want the suppliers to invest in technology that will allow the organisation to provide a quality platform, high level of customer service, availability of spare parts and information exchange. Suppliers would be more willing to invest in assets if they feel that they have a relationship with an organisation. As suggested earlier, a decrease in uncertainty with improved supplier relationships will encourage suppliers to invest more money into buying assets that will enhance the value provided by the buying organisation.

There are enabling technologies that allow organisations to better connect with organisations and determine the outcome of relationships. Linkages such as EDI reduce costs for both customers and suppliers and dramatically reduce lead times. Also, with improved technology, organisations can customise their offerings to individual customers. Researchers suggest that there should be multi-tiered offerings for customers with customers self-selecting a level of service based on their purchase behaviour.

This trend toward differential offerings is expected to increase. There are information systems available that allow organisations to determine the profitability of each customers of an organisation. Information technology also allows marketers to cater to the need of individual customers (that is each customer can receive a customised offering). In an environment of ever increasing competition, organisations would wish to retain the more profitable customers at a cost of losing the less profitable customers.

The consequence of better customer information and ability to customise offerings can lead to a higher level of customer selectivity. The consequence of customer selectivity will manifest itself into better customers getting better offerings than marginal customers. The trend toward determining and catering to the needs of profitable customers has major implications for marginal customers or customers that are only average.

If business marketers provide differential offerings to different customers, some businesses may have a resource-based advantage over their competitors. Thus, it may be in an organisation's advantage to be a better customer and receive additional services.

Supply chain relationships increase competitiveness by locking in good suppliers. Today, intense competition is coming from existing rivals, new entrants and the threat of substitutes. Relationships with suppliers can be an effective method of reducing competition's negative impact in an industry.

The emphasis of a relationship orientation toward suppliers will lead to an exploration of the following aspects:

- *Supplier as customer*. There will be a thrust toward developing and maintaining relationships with customers. We have identified areas of commitment, trust, cooperation, mutual goals, interdependence, performance satisfaction, structural bonds, adaptation, non-retrievable investments, shared technology and social bonds as antecedents to successful relationships.

- *Cross-functional supplier teams*. As individual suppliers' relationships become more important, we can expect a thrust toward cross-functional teams that are dedicated on their key suppliers. The importance of individual suppliers is expected to increase because of the emergence of sourcing on a global and relational basis. However, as these cross-functional supplier teams replace the buying centre structure and process, there will be a need for applying existing knowledge, frameworks, concepts and methods to enhance performance of cross-functional supplier teams.

Improving supplier relationships: Implementation difficulties

A study by Stuart and McCutcheon examined a different issue: potential sources of problems in establishing such relationships with suppliers, which is an area of investigation that has largely been ignored. The study compares perceptual differences between matched samples of buyers and suppliers concerning their interrelationships. Specifically examined are partnerships in which suppliers perceive the relationship less positively than do their buyer counterparts, based on suspected reasons that might lead to suppliers' lower assessment of their arrangements.

STRATEGIC SUPPLIER PARTNERSHIPS

Prior research has contrasted the partnership style of relationship with the traditional approach for dealing with suppliers, a relationship characterised by low commitment, limited information sharing and contractual delineation of each party's role.

While transaction-type arrangements are suitable in many circumstances, some authors have suggested that competitive bidding is not the preferred supplier selection method when, among other reasons, issues other than price (for example, quality or technical capability) are of major concern. Drawbacks to the competitive bidding process have been discussed extensively by a number of authors.

Typically, a partnership is characterised by a buyer providing more information about order quantities and timing, upcoming design changes, long-range plans and sometimes about process technology assistance. At the same time, the supplier usually becomes more involved in product design and in providing broader technical support to the buyer. In return, the buyer usually commits a larger share of its business over an agreed period of time exclusively to the supplier partner.

MATCH AND MISMATCH OF PERCEPTIONS

Depending on circumstances, organisations may have differing opportunities and capabilities to establish broader terms for their relationships with suppliers. Therefore, a partnership can be viewed as a matter of degree of mutual involvement. The degree of collaboration can be measured by assessing two characteristics that are considered hallmarks of the non-traditional arrangement:

- the amount of joint problem solving;
- the equality in benefit sharing that occurs.

Organisations reporting higher levels of these characteristics are considered to have a greater degree of partnership.

Measuring the degree of alliance in this way can also reveal problems in the purchasing arrangement. The views of both buyer and supplier can be sought independently and compared. There are three possible outcomes from buyer–supplier comparisons:

- The supplier and buyer may agree on the degree of collaboration that is present, regardless of whether it is high or low.
- The supplier may see a strong collaboration, but the buyer may not believe that such a partnership exists.
- The buyer may see a strong collaboration, while the supplier believes it to be otherwise.

The perceptual matching can be represented by the matrix presented in Figure 4.3.

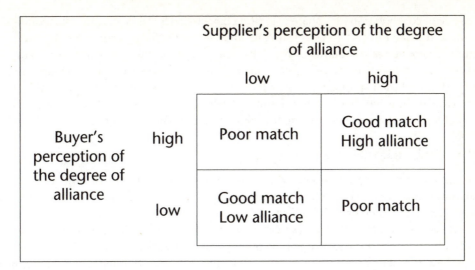

Figure 4.3   Possible buyer–supplier alliance perceptions

The match of the buyer–supplier perceptions – that is, into which quadrant they fall, might have significant impacts on the effectiveness in dealing with suppliers.

If both the buying company and its supplier agree that theirs is a low collaboration, traditional-style relationship (lower left quadrant), then each will act accordingly, likely with arm's-length, price-driven transactions and little information or benefit sharing. If both parties agree that theirs is a relationship with a high degree of supplier collaboration (upper right quadrant), then both the procurement department and the supplier organisations have met their respective goals of establishing a different transactional basis.

However, the mismatches represent potentially intriguing or difficult situations. If the supplier perceives a high degree of collaboration while the buyer does not (lower right quadrant), then the buying organisation is achieving desired results without necessarily providing what it perceives as much information, technical help or benefits. Such situations represent opportunities whereby the benefits and gains of collaboration are being achieved by the buying company without the pain associated with introducing collaboration management. Buyers would be particularly interested in whether such illusionary partnerships are sustainable and whether or not the benefits accrued are equivalent to those situations requiring more extensive involvement.

On the other hand, if the purchaser perceives they are collaborating more than the supplier does (upper left quadrant), the purchaser may have a poor idea about how the organisation's efforts to establish supplier collaboration were viewed by its partners. There could be significant implications if the buying organisation fails to recognise that its efforts to build collaboration through greater information and benefit sharing leave its supplier unimpressed. Such situations could lead upset suppliers to switch their offerings as well as their accrued knowledge, including process improvements and new technical skills, to other buying organisations.

OVERESTIMATION OF AN ALLIANCE BY THE PURCHASER

There are several reasons why a supplier might report a lower degree of collaboration than its buyer counterpart (the upper left quadrant). One such reason is that suppliers who disagree about the degree of collaboration may share common characteristics. There may be prior conditions that make it more difficult to establish collaborative relationships with some suppliers, for example, the policy of not allowing any collaborative approaches due to fears of corruptive practices, and so on. Alternatively, some buyers may implement their relationship building in ways that lead their suppliers to take a more negative view of the supposed collaboration. In one case, the mismatch relates to the supplier selection procedures, while the latter case is attributable to mismanagement during the contract and the relationship itself.

PERCEPTUAL MISMATCHES

Certain conditions may predispose some suppliers to judge a relationship as less of a collaborative one: conditions such as relative size or power, perceived ability to gain something through the relationship or willingness to deal openly with the purchaser.

There is a belief that the subject of negotiation is a 'zero-sum game' and that advantages to one party accrue only at the expense of the other party. Such situations would be characterised by large amounts of mistrust and suspicion, efforts to block goal attainment of the other party and the use of coercive power to exercise influence.

There are other situations in which each party believes that the other can influence outcomes and that a healthy degree of information sharing occurs. The basic assumption about collaboration is that the arrangement is based on a 'win–win' relationship, in which both parties are better off from the negotiated arrangement than they would otherwise have been.

Some suppliers may view the world from a 'win–lose' mindset, regardless of a purchaser's attempts to offer a different relationship. Companies that use their dominant position as buyers to force supplier collaboration will be viewed negatively by suppliers. Similarly, buying organisations that say they have collaboration but do not have technical resources for the associated supplier improvement efforts will be viewed negatively by the supplier organisations.

CONCLUSIONS AND MANAGEMENT IMPLICATIONS

There is clear evidence that failure to meet suppliers' expectations, either because the expectations were too high or because the delivery did not meet expected values, as well as withholding information necessary for problem solving, creates conflict.

In summary, purchasing managers can enhance their chances of success in collaboration building by seeking organisations that are philosophically well matched for non-transactional-type relationships: by communicating the advantages from such collaboration to the supplier; and by ensuring that information and technical assistance is available. Both the selection procedure and the collaboration process are critical in ensuring success.

To enhance the prospects for success in establishing supplier collaboration, customers should design and implement an operating plan similar to the one noted below:

- Identify supplier organisations in which a philosophical match exists between the two organisations' managements on such issues as views toward quality and productivity improvement. Such a fit is possible despite differences in the parties' sizes and power.
- Create an intercompany task force to establish clear expectations of the information required for successful problem identification and resolution, the level of technical expertise available from both parties, and how the benefits from such improvements are to be measured and then shared in a mutually agreeable manner.
- Slightly exceed the expectations established in the bullet point above.

CASE STUDY
ZENECA – CHANGING RELATIONSHIPS: INDIVIDUALS, TEAMS AND COMPANY CULTURES

Zeneca was the first organisation to receive a commemorative plaque from Aalco, the multi-metal distribution arm of Glynwed Metal Services, signifying that they had concluded a trading relationship agreement of major significance. This marked a new relationship between the two companies that offers benefits for both parties. It also sheds light on the difficulties of forging a close working relationships and the development of Zeneca's new style of procurement.

With a total spend of around £2 billion, Zeneca also inherited approximately 35 000 global suppliers which the company had begun to pare sharply to get better value for money. Although not actively looking for partnership-type arrangements with suppliers, they were nonetheless an important feature of Zeneca procurement.

Zeneca's Engineering Procurement Manager preferred the title 'trading relationship agreement' to the word 'partnership', believing that 'partnership' smacked of a cosy relationship, adding to the many false beliefs about such relationships.

Aalco was the first supplier to develop a close trading relationship with Zeneca, after moves to single sourcing as part of Zeneca's policy of trimming its supply base. From dealing with some 30 suppliers of stainless steel, the company concentrated instead solely on getting supplies from Aalco.

The relationship has however become much more than simply single sourcing, as Zeneca now no longer carries any stocks of stainless steel and draws its supplies directly from Aalco. Furthermore, Zeneca has achieved control over the materials used by its third-party sub-contractors and fabricators.

Although relations between the two companies have now been set on a course of working closer together, the presentation ceremony is seen as only really the starting point for future, deeper cooperation.

Getting to this point was far from easy, though, and took a lot of hard work, involving nearly 24 months of detailed discussions. There were doubts on both sides about being able to hammer out an even-handed relationship. Eventually, however, a meeting of minds was achieved.

Probably the biggest obstacle was the trust factor, as it meant taking a big step from the common adversarial relationship: 'Before you can put your cards on the table, there has to be a level of trust, particularly in providing information.' The relationship does though mean a sharing in the financial bottom line.

Although there are sound commercial advantages for both companies, including retaining the position of sole supplier for Aalco and cost savings for Zeneca, the Engineering Procurement Manager says that the relationship is 'robust' enabling a number of difficulties to be overcome.

One of the biggest barriers to closer trading relationships is spreading the necessary culture change throughout the organisation. It takes time for the message to get through and to change past practices. The benefits are so apparent however that both companies have begun to adopt similar relationships with other organisations.

For the present the new relationship is regarded as a joint commitment, involving an exchange of ideas and 'is a better way of doing things'.

Levels of communications

As we have seen earlier, 'trust' can be defined as, 'reliably doing what you would do'.

If this philosophy is applied continually in a cooperative style, then relationships over time will move inexorably from win/lose towards more respectful attitudes and onwards into win/win scenarios. As Figure 4.4 (from *The Seven Habits of Highly Effective People* by S. Covey) indicates, this is a continual process over time and requires a continued effort in terms of adopting approaches which build in trust-building actions and cooperative stances.

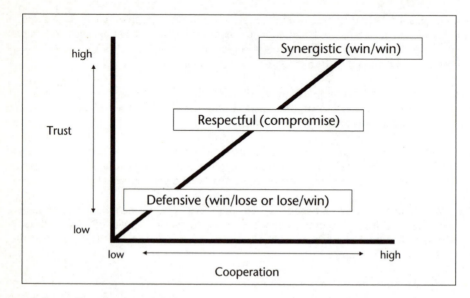

Figure 4.4   Trust/cooperation

Therefore again we must emphasise the need for a longer-term perspective over which such cooperation can flourish, with the accompanying benefit stream. The above Zeneca case study makes the same point.

The following case study further emphasises the role of communication.

CASE STUDY

ND MARSTON – DEVELOPING VENDOR RELATIONSHIPS: 'WORKING TOGETHER'

ND Marston is based in Shipley, West Yorkshire. This case study is intended to record the progress over the past three years and focus on two important areas: vendor relations and working together.

Introduction
ND Marston design and manufacture heat exchange units, radiators and intercoolers for the automotive industry. They started down the path of an MRPII system (Material Requirements Planning II – a developments of the original MRP approach) and the first blocks for success were in place:

- education
- quality
- lead time
- training
- data accuracy
- delivery.

Performance measurement and disciplines generated the benefits and ND Marston became an A-class MRPII company. This was one of the many steps towards becoming a world-class company. They then realised that they must concentrate solely on two areas:

- vendor relationships
- working together.

Their vendor development programme began with supplier education, which started with vendor days to:

- improve quality performance;
- improve delivery performance;
- improve lead times;
- develop a long-term agreement.

Every two weeks, a one-day vendor day was arranged by inviting three or more representatives from five or more suppliers to their Shipley Works. Procurement, with guest speakers from Quality and Design, hosted the visit. The days were open and friendly, and at the end of each vendor day the suppliers understood how ND Marston's MRPII system would work, with new schedules layout and how good quality and on-time deliveries were imperative for the MRPII to work.

The Quality Department discussed how supplier rejects were recorded and what actions should be taken. This extended to quality and delivery performance measurement, which were posted to each supplier every month. Each supplier was given the opportunity to have a one-to-one discussion at the end of each day.

The vendor days were very good, a success, better than expected. A questionnaire was handed to all suppliers, asking for updates of their products, personnel, finances, equipped manufacturing facilities, quality systems and customers.

Early improvements were:

- lead-time reduction after vendor day;
- improved proportion of suppliers achieving 95 per cent on-time deliveries;
- reduced inventory levels.

As the vendor days continued, the quality and delivery performance measurements generated benefits. The vendor programme continued and included the following:

- vendor improvement plan;
- working together (team work);
- design, quality, manufacturing, suppliers, scheduling and delivery;
- daily deliveries, smaller quantities.

They re-addressed the vendor days and invited the top ten vendors to open days. This was a huge success and was attended by two or more senior personnel from each supplier. The agenda included:

- ND Marston annual report;
- summary of their 5-year plan;
- current position;
- future actions, countermeasures and targets.

An area that is sometimes forgotten or left out are vendor days for overseas suppliers. Mid year, they invited their German suppliers to attend such an event and had a very good day.

Update visits
The update visits provided a good example of teamwork. Personnel from the Quality, Design, Production and Procurement Departments visit a supplier to present the ND Marston report, a summary of the 5-year plan, and the company's current position. They would discuss supplier progress, lead time, quality, design, delivery and scrap reduction. The agenda would be the same for each vendor. A lot of the time was spent with each individual supplier in order to understand their production and breakdown of the lead time at this supplier.

Review
ND Marston reviewed their vendor relationship programme – could it work better? They reduced the number of suppliers, which showed vast improvements in quality and delivery, setting the scene for the future and improving the relationship between customer and supplier.

Introducing new products
In the past, new products were late, programmes were late or parts were late. Traditionally, the supplier would have no lead times or have a secondary role. But with a new start, a new position using a project manager and teamwork, and giving responsibility to design and development meant bringing into production a new product on time and getting it right first time. An important element of this new team is including the supplier at the concept design stage.

The first product using this team, with the supplier being involved from the start, was sampled and the results to date are very good.

Relationships are now even better and the top suppliers meet at the Shipley site on a monthly basis. The agenda covers an update on the current position, future actions, countermeasures and targets. Quality, design and deliveries are also reviewed.

Relationships on the quality front have improved due to weekly supply quality assurance visits. As part of their efforts in working together, ND Marston visits suppliers' works with a party of five or six in order to understand the product, how it is made and where it is made. The team includes design, quality, sales, production operators and procurement.

Summary
Working together with suppliers is not a soft option. It is hard work but the benefits are there to be enjoyed. What ND Marston have achieved to date with their suppliers has come through improved communication initiatives.

Collaboration: Perspectives

This section is based upon a Centre for Advanced Purchasing Studies (CAPS) focus study (1989) looking simultaneously at the perceptions of both buyers and suppliers who mutually agree that they are involved in a partnership. It explores the impetus for entering the partnership, as well as the key success factors and factors contributing to failure in previous partnering relationships. It provides useful insights into the similarities and differences in buyers' and suppliers' perceptions.

'Partnering' is defined here as, 'an ongoing relationship between two organisations which involves a commitment over an extended time period, and a mutual sharing of the risks and rewards of the relationship'.

This study provides a contribution beyond much of the previous research in that it looks at the issues associated with buyer–supplier partnering from the perspective of both the buyer and the supplier simultaneously.

Here, we shall attempt to answer:

- Why do buyers and suppliers become involved in partnering relationships?
- What are the key issues that make those relationships a success?
- When previous partnering relationships have not worked out, what have been the key factors that contributed to that failure?

By definition, a partnership relationship is a two-way relationship involving a mutual exchange of ideas, information and benefits. Yet, limited research has been done to explore whether there is truly a meeting of the minds in successful relationships, and what the current perceptions of the participants reflect.

In addition, it is of interest to find out why partnerships fail from the perspectives of both the buyer and the seller, particularly to obtain some insight from the perspectives of buyers and suppliers who have been able to make such partnering relationships succeed under different circumstances.

Why do buyers and suppliers enter into collaborative relationships? We will look into both perspectives.

BUYER'S PERSPECTIVE

As indicated in the table below, the two primary reasons that buying organisations enter partnerships are to obtain a better price or total cost for the purchased item and to secure a reliable source. Price/cost has long been a driving force in traditional buyer–supplier relationships, so it is not surprising that this is still a critical issue.

Main reasons why companies enter collaborative relationships	Rank
Price of delivery item	1
Secure reliable sources	2
Influencing supplier's quality	3
Improve delivery schedules	4
Access to supplier's new technology	5
Reduce internal procurement procedures and costs	6
Support JIT initiatives	7
Reduce administration procedures and costs (for example, ordering and invoicing)	8

Source reliability is a broad factor, which encompasses the idea of having an ensured source of supply in times of scarcity, a source that will live up to its commitments and promises, and one that exhibits overall dependability. Again, it is not surprising that this was a very crucial factor in seeking out a long-term relationship with a supplier.

The ability to influence supplier quality was the third-ranked factor, followed closely by the desire to influence supplier delivery schedules. Price, quality and delivery traditionally have been the three most important supplier selection factors; it is not surprising to see a continuation of these priorities.

SUPPLIER'S PERSPECTIVE

The supplier's perspective is summarised below.

Main reasons why suppliers enter collaborative relationships	Rank
Secure buyer for product	1
Influence customer's quality	2
Support customer's JIT intiatives	3
Improve forecasts of requirements	4
Reduce ongoing administration	5
Reduce internal sales procedures and costs (for example, preparing RFQs)	6
Price improvement	7
Influence/gain access to customer's new technology	8

Not surprisingly, the number one reason that suppliers enter partnership arrangements is to secure a reliable market for a given product. The buyers also saw this corresponding element as important, and rated the ability to secure a reliable source as their second most important factor. Suppliers indicated that desire to influence customer quality was the second most important motivator to enter a partnership. However, it was significantly less important than the acquisition of a reliable market.

One of the biggest gaps between buyers and suppliers in rankings of importance was related to the JIT initiative. The suppliers ranked this as third, whilst the buyers ranked it as seventh in importance. Clearly, suppliers see the buyer organisation's drive towards a JIT initiative as a much more important issue in partnership than the buyers do.

Another big difference in responses between buyers and suppliers is in the area of administration procedures. Suppliers see reduction of ongoing administration procedures as a more important reason to enter a partnership than do buyers.

The most interesting difference in the partnering impetus relates to the pricing aspect of partnering arrangements. Price and total cost was the key driver for buyers to form a partnership, ranking first.

However, suppliers appear not to be as concerned with the price received as they are with having reliable demand, influencing quality, supporting JIT and obtaining better requirements forecasts. Thus, suppliers are also considering the 'total cost to do business with an organisation' in their selection of partners.

Key factors for establishing successful collaborative relationships

Here we analyse perceptions of the key factors necessary to establish and maintain viable collaborative relationships. Note that the five factors with the highest ratings for buyers are:

- two-way information sharing;
- top management support;
- shared goals;
- early communication to suppliers;
- supplier adds distinctive value.

It is interesting to note below how important almost all of the success factors surveyed are perceived to be by both groups.

Important factors in establishing and maintaining collaborative relationships	Buyers' response (rank)	Suppliers' response (rank)
Two-way information sharing	1	2
Top management support	2	1
Shared goals	3	6
Early communication (specification changes)	4	11
Supplier adds distinctive value	5	3
Flexibility in agreement	6	10
TQM initiative	7	4
Training in partnership philosophies	8	14

Important factors in establishing and maintaining collaborative relationships	Buyers' response (rank)	Suppliers' response (rank)
Site visits to suppliers	9	12
Multiple relationships or points of contact	10	8
Sharing examples of success	11	16
Ongoing relationship between top levels	12	7
Rewards/recognition for progress	13	13
Personal relationships	14	9
Compatible corporate cultures	15	15
Establishing a task force	16	17
JIT initiative	17	5

WHY DO COLLABORATIVE RELATIONSHIPS FAIL?

Respondents were asked to reflect on previous collaborative relationships that did not reach full potential or had to be dissolved. The results are displayed below:

Factors contributing to failed collaborations	Buyers' response (rank)	Suppliers' response (rank)
Poor communication	1	1
Lack of top management support	2	10
Lack of trust	3	4
Lack of total quality commitment by supplier	4	18
Poor upfront planning	5	5
Lack of distinctive value-added quality/benefit	6	13
Lack of strategic direction	7	3
Lack of shared goals	8	2
Ineffective mechanism for conflict resolution	9	7
Lack of benefit/risk sharing	10	6
Agreement does not support a partnership philosophy	11	9
Partner organisation lacks top support	12	8
Changes in the market	13	16
Supplier base too large	14	15
Corporate culture differences	15	17
Top management differences	16	14
Lack of central purchasing	17	12
Low status of purchasing	18	11
Distance barriers	19	19

(After Ellram, L. (1995) in *International Journal of Project Management*, Vol.31/2, pp. 10–16)

First, poor communication ranked as the most important cause of collaborative relationships failure for both groups. Also important to both groups were lack of trust, poor upfront planning and lack of shared goals.

Suppliers saw lack of central coordination of the buyer's purchasing function as a significantly more important factor in failure than did the buyers. Other interesting issues that suppliers saw as significantly more important in contributing to partnering failure than buyers include a lack of strategic direction of the relationship and a lack of shared goals. Perhaps the suppliers saw these as more important because the buyer generally takes a leadership role in buyer–supplier relationships. The suppliers were thus relying on the buyers to provide the strategic direction, and share the goals that support that strategy. Suppliers also saw a lack of benefit/risk sharing as a much more important cause of dissolution of partnerships than did buyers.

Suppliers also viewed the lack of a buyer's top management support as a relatively more important factor in partnership failure than the lack of their own top management support. Buyers agreed that their top management was a much more important contributor to collaborative relationships failure than was the supplier's top management.

The only items buyers considered significantly more important in contributing to the relationship dissolution than the suppliers were lack of distinctive value added benefits by the supplier and lack of a total quality commitment by the supplier.

This information can be quite useful for suppliers who should probably place more emphasis on their quality and distinctive value-added performance. These differences in perception can well be important factors to consider when developing, maintaining or enhancing partnerships.

The items considered being relatively unimportant to failure to both buyer and supplier includes distance barriers, top management differences, too many suppliers, corporate culture differences and changes in the market.

The following amplify many of the above points:

VIEWPOINT
CHANGING NHS PURCHASING

The following is seen as needed:

- Change the purchasing structure, promote the best staff and encourage new employees to adopt modern ideas and gain experience of up-to-date buying techniques.
- Change the purchasing systems, so that administration is more streamlined and information is more accessible.
- Most importantly, change the attitude and culture, so that everyone with supplier contact – not just those in purchasing – understands the main implications of their behaviour and how their actions affect the way their suppliers respond and behave towards them.

(Based on: 'Heart of the Matter', *Supply Management*, 15 June 2000, by Will Parsons)

CASE STUDY
CHANGING SUPPLY RELATIONSHIPS

The company:

- subcontractor in manufacturing;
- used TQM principles inside the company;
- looked at supply base and found 12 suppliers provided 80 per cent of materials;
- investigated single supplier route for this 80 per cent.

Way forward:

- held a supplier day;
- explained TQM;
- explained the 'single sources' would gain business;
- advised on requirements of openness, trust, clear joint objectives and continuous improvements that involved all suppliers staff;
- supplier selection criteria were:
  - TQM culture 30 per cent;
  - quality 25 per cent;
  - on-time delivery 25 per cent;
  - price 20 per cent using total acquisition cost principles.

Supplier commitment involved:

- implicit trust with no inspection;
- Kanban supply (two bin, minimum once per week supplier visit/replenishment);
- one invoice per month and paid immediately.

Benefits found for manufacturer/customer:

- secure supply;
- delivery reliability;
- improved quality;
- purchase activity reduced.

Benefits found for suppliers:

- freedom to perform;
- paid on time;
- longer planning horizons;
- financial stability.

Other findings:

- 'Constantly surprised at the resistance to change.'

It is noted that the resistance to change was a 'constant surprise'; therefore the topic of managing change will now therefore be examined.

Managing change

As noted above, resistance to change should be expected. Change is one of the constants of modern life; the only certain aspect of the future is that it will be different – a future of stable turbulence. It is in dealing with this uncertainty in the future that managing change becomes a key management function. Managing change also involves the full and complete management repertoire; unfortunately it is estimated that the majority of change fails; which also says something about the quality of the management involved.

SOURCES OF CHANGE

There are many sources of change and some of these general categories are as follows. Some of these may well sponsor the adoption of better supply chain relationships:

- political, for example trade agreements;
- economic, for example currency fluctuations and inflation levels;
- social, for example lifestyles and increased leisure;
- technological, for example ICT;
- legal, for example legislation;
- organisational, for example takeovers, closures and new start ups.

Additionally most people will have noticed the following trends and resultant changes in recent times:

From old ways	Towards new ways
Technology/product/supply	Customer/market/demand
'Push' product flows	'Pull' product flows
Product sells	Customer buys
Manage people	Manage messages
Specialist skills	Broad skills
Bureaucratic control	Empowerment
Instruction/telling	Consulting/selling
Job for life	Portfolio jobs
Earning a living	Learning a living
Adversarial	Partnership
Fire-fighting	Fire-lighting
'If it isn't broke then don't fix it'	'Let's improve it'

REACTIONS TO CHANGE

Change can be dramatic and can, if handled wrongly, be traumatic enough to cause a company to fail. Change will almost always impact on people at some time. The impact will vary, but all those involved will experience and go through identical stages, usually however, at different times. The following table shows the stages involved with some typical responses. Stage 1 commences when a person first hears about the change.

Stage		Comments	'Here' to 'there'
1	Shock, immobilised	'They cannot do it'	Past orientation
2	Denial	'We will never do it'	Past
3	Frustration and defensive	'It is just too difficult'	Past
4	Acceptance and discarding	'I might try'	Past/future
5	Testing	'Lets try'	Future
6	Search for meaning	'It seems to work'	Future
7	Integration	'I can do it'	Future

People's attitudes to change will therefore vary in any group of people. These attitudes can be very emotional and wide ranging:

- stimulating to resisting;
- exciting to denying;
- dynamic to fear;
- anticipation to anger;
- enthusiastic to stress;
- exciting to concern;
- challenging to worry;
- opportunity to certainty;
- visionary to staying with the current situation.

It is critical to appreciate that all people will go through such emotional responses, but they do it differently and at different times. Managers need to be alert to such variations and to manage them effectively, remember that people have to cope and deal with changes one at a time.

Resistance to change can however be minimised when:

- it is agreed by all;
- it is owned by individuals;
- it is supported by management;
- it follows culture and values;
- it decreases current problems;
- it increases new experiences and interests;
- emotions are understood by management;
- reactions are allowed to be discussed with management;
- it does not cause personal security to be threatened.

The dynamics of change are found in any change situation. There are two forces dynamically involved, the driving and the restraining forces.

Examples of driving forces are:

- job enrichment
- upgrading
- broadening

- more responsibility
- more reward
- more status
- better conditions
- easier work.

Examples of restraining forces are:

- de-skilling
- no discretion
- changed jobs
- more difficult work
- degrading
- no promotions
- redundancy

One force represents the 'foot on the gas', whilst the other one represents the 'foot on the brake'. A key action therefore is to identify the driving forces (and the backers) and the restraining forces (and the blockers) in a change situation. Next is to recognise that if we move forward by increasing the driving forces, then resistance may well increase to maintain the balance. Consequently, the best way to move forward is by analysing the restraining forces and trying to minimise their impact.

CHANGE AND COMMUNICATION

Managing change is a skilful process, and a key skill in dealing with change is communication. It has been said that communication and change are synonymous as people are fearful and are uncertain and therefore need to be communicated with clearly. This communication will involve the following:

- Don't 'tell' propaganda, but 'sell' proper communication.
- Inform at all stages.
- Ask questions to uncover feeling.
- Listen carefully to answers.
- Use written communications only where appropriate. Concentrate mainly, on face-to-face methods.
- Consult wherever possible.
- Admit any mistakes and learn from them.
- Celebrate individuals and group success.
- Be as open as you can.

Communication is not a one-off exercise but is continual: during change it should be communicate, communicate, communicate. It is critical to involve people – communicate, listen, give people chance to air objections and give people time to adapt.

Communicating involves sharing information between people, up and down and side to side, with the objective being to prevent misunderstanding. The dictionary defines communication as 'the process of conveying, imparting or exchanging information'. Unfortunately much of what passes for communication is actually one way and no attempt is made, either, to check on whether it has been understood, as demonstrated by one FTSE 100 company who renamed all their notice boards 'communication boards'. (The former description was the correct one.) In order for communication to be effective, it is not sufficient simply to transmit a message; it must be received and be understood.

The following questions focus on how communication should actually work in a company:

- Is there evidence of an interchange of ideas?
- Do employees know the reasons for the job they are being asked to do?
- Can changes be introduced without major upsets?
- Are ideas used that are put forward and if not, is it explained why?
- Are those nearest to the job consulted on matters affecting them?
- Are new employees carefully inducted?
- Do all people know what their jobs are?
- Do people show a sustained interest in their jobs?
- Is there a smooth flow of work?
- Are people seldom bypassed in the flow of information?
- Is the 'grapevine' a very small one?
- Does the manager walk round at least once a day?
- Do the managers know where to go for answers to their people's questions?
- Do the managers clearly understand their responsibilities and those of others?
- Do the managers have good working relationships with colleagues?
- Do the managers know all your people by name?

People's behaviour during change

As we have noted earlier in 'Team relationships', people change one at a time. The following acts as a reminder to that section on team building, and shows how people react, how they change and how that change will occur with different people at different times.

It will be recalled that the stages involved were:

- 'forming' and starting out;
- 'storming' and getting together;
- 'norming' and getting understanding;
- 'performing' and going well;
- 'mourning' and ending.

Each stage has specific emotions and behaviours and these were fully commented upon earlier.

THE IMPORTANCE OF THE 'STORMING' STEP

The above steps will occur in the order shown. It will be noticed that the steps, from starting out to performing, involves going though 'storming' and 'getting together' and that this storming step involves handling conflict amongst people.

This is an important step and will nearly always be involved. How this step is handled therefore, will determine the onward progress towards norming, performing and eventual success. It is a step that should not be dismissed but one that is dealt with carefully and maturely. This will require leaders who will:

- cultivate trust;
- take responsibility;
- be open;
- be consistent;
- speak from the emotional heart as well as using 'head logic';
- have integrity;
- use power positively;
- confront without being confrontational (there is a role for using conflict and challenge when dealing with people's behaviour).

It is often said that perception is reality. Words and the way they are used can sometimes be perceived by the sender as being a constructive challenge to a way of thinking or doing. However, because of the words used, or the way they are expressed, the receiver may perceive them as being hurtful with the potential that they could lead to conflict.

Conflict here should mean the conflict of ideas, and not conflict between people. It is an open disagreement on ideas. It is not a conflict involving verbal aggression (or for that matter, any other types of aggression).

The following case study will help to clarify this view of conflict:

CASE STUDY
CONFLICT

When talking with employees of carmakers in different parts of the world, researchers noticed that some employees said they avoided conflict whenever possible in product development discussions, while others seemed to thrive on conflict in much the same circumstances. To confuse the researchers even further, those who seemed positive about conflict seemed to perform better in many respects in their product development (and overall organisational performance) than those who discussed conflict negatively.

Probing further, the researchers found that different people (and organisations) used the term conflict in very different ways:

- For those who perceived conflict as negative, conflict was personalised and represented destructive personal tensions.
- For those who viewed conflict as positive, conflict was simply an intellectual disagreement to be resolved and had no relation at all with their feelings about the other party.

The first approach can be called conflict among people (or destructive conflict) and the latter, conflict of ideas (or constructive conflict).

Some people do not like the word conflict: it is associated with aggravation and unease between people. However, this is just one possible side of conflict for, as the above case study shows, conflict has two sides: one that is both creative and constructive, and one that is feared and destructive.

When conflict is creative and positive, it:

- explores differences and does not concentrate on only one position;
- allows for constructive criticism that can build up to a newly discovered third position;
- means that both parties may each concede, so that they both will gain;
- develops a common cause, a relationship with tough trust, and where truth will come from debate and discussion amongst equals.

When conflict is feared and negative, it can be that:

- at least one side has taken it personally (this will often happen where one side has not treated the other as an equal);
- unresolved differences go on to create stand-offs. This can continue into destructive outcomes, and perhaps end with one party deciding to take their ball and bat home (whoever said that grown-ups are children in disguise, maybe has a point);
- people withdraw and curl up into their shell;
- people may well comply, and go along with things for the sake of peace (t least they may do this when they are face to face, but they will often behave differently behind each other's back).

USING CHALLENGE AND COMPLIANCE

When two people discuss and face each other, without any challenge, there will only ever be an outcome of compliance. This compliance may be acceptable, if it is has followed on from a dialogue of constructive criticism and it is genuine and agreed by both parties.

However, positive challenge will be needed:

- if there is to be any learning and changing;
- when people have to talk about touchy subjects, as then they can talk openly without being defensive;
- if there is a need to open any discussion using questioning and reflection;
- to explore and perhaps see the other's point of view;
- to modify our own position.

This type of challenge is positive as it helps and benefits both parties to develop and to learn.

However, with forced or negative compliance, developing and learning is hindered and the following result:

- There is no learning, as there can be no change.
- It can exist amongst unequal partners where one of the parties does not want to rock the boat.
- People will learn to keep quiet and cover up anything that will put their head over the parapet and expose them.
- People will defend themselves by hiding away and keeping a safe distance.
- Mistakes will also be hidden (as this is no place to be where you can learn from mistakes).
- Furthermore, forced compliance can be covert with unspoken disagreement.

Consider the following case study on negative compliance:

CASE STUDY
NEGATIVE COMPLIANCE

The managing director of a successful component manufacturer has a very simple human resources policy: hire winners and fire losers. In practice being seen as a loser by the MD means demotion or at worst termination. Unfortunately, this MD is on a rather short fuse and any employee seen making a mistake will always be a loser. Consequently, the clever employees learnt many astute ways of covering up failures, even when they were genuine ones. As a result, problems tend to appear too late, when nothing can be done about them. The MD then has to step in, fix them as he can and look for a scapegoat. He keeps complaining that he spends his time fire-fighting rather than dealing with fundamental strategic issues.

In this case study there has been no positive challenge and conflict. Therefore, there is no opening of differences, which are essential to new learning as they represent an opportunity to learn and see something new.

With positive challenge and conflict, each party will aim for a mutual awareness of differences. Without it, negative compliance results.

The employees in the above case study for example are fostering negative compliance. This is likely because they do not like the personal conflict, which they see as being destructive. Also, the MD is fostering negative compliance through his personal style and approach, although he probably does not realise this.

To summarise therefore on challenge/conflict and compliance:

Positive conflict

- It is constructive as it enables new learning through an open disagreement and discussion on ideas between people.
- The outcome is either a full agreement about the other's position (there has been a 'we' view and a 'walking in each others shoes'); or
- The outcome is a new, third position (through taking an emotional detachment and an objective helicopter view).
- All those involved believe they have gained something from the conflict process.

Negative conflict

- It is destructive as it inhibits new learning through creating personal tensions among people.
- The outcome is a single 'my' view.
- The position taken is essentially founded on an emotional subjective response.
- Those involved are usually divided, as, whilst one may feel they have gained, the other may feel they have lost.

Positive compliance

- It encourages challenge and positive conflicts and recognises that these are needed for effective learning and changing.
- People are actively involved in shaping the outcome from a mutual awareness and understanding of the differences.
- People can change their position in the process.

Negative compliance

- It encourages blind or forced agreement which hinders effective learning and changing.
- It discourages open challenge and positive conflict on any differences from the status quo.
- One party remains uninvolved and keeps quiet with unspoken disagreement. (This gives a false agreement, which can encourage mistakes to be repeated, and little change brought to the status quo.)
- People will internally remain with their own position, even though this will not be externally expressed in their false agreement.

In forming a team and starting out together, people can seek to establish that the purpose of being together is for learning, changing and improving. To do this effectively agreement is not always required and disagreements are healthy in developing understanding, learning and change.

Finally, if the storming behaviour is dismissed, then the underlying emotions will be suppressed, possibly reappearing later in an uncontrolled way. People do therefore need to be allowed to express their feelings and opinions in the storming step.

However, readers who remain unconvinced about change and making paradigm shifts, should review the following:

Paradigm shifts (or 'Look what has changed')

Old paradigm	New paradigm
Factory model with cheap and plentiful standard products for a mass market	Craft inventive model with bespoke products for an experience and fashion-driven economy
Manager is the technical expert	All are experts
Behaviourism with reward/punishment	Empowerment
Central and bureaucratic control	Organic, self- and fluid controls
Competitive approaches	Collaborative approaches
Brain is logical	Brain is also emotional
Narrow problems/solutions	Global problems/holistic solutions
Cost reduction	Service/value enhancement

This demonstrates very simply the changes that have been seen and are still ongoing. Staying with one view can be dangerous in a self-changing and moving world.

The following comments are some eternal reminders on change:

Checklist: Changing supplier relationships and moving inventory

The following comments were made by senior people:

On paper, the process seems simple to implement, but in the real world of personalities and professional relationships, there are many obstacles to climb. Trust is very important to succeed.

For years and years buyers have been trained not to disclose information to vendors. You play one vendor off another, and its all part of the card game. So trying to get through years of accumulated baggage is tough.

Better relationships mean less inventory sitting in a warehouse and there is no value in excess inventory.

Personal relationships that bridge former gaps in communications between vendor and retailer are what can really spell success.

It changes the paradigm. It's definitely a different type of relationship with your customer. It's based on mutual trust and it's got to be there to succeed.

Employees, especially salespeople and buyers, can be a particularly hard sell. Salespeople need to change their attitude about 'piling it high and watching it fly'. The goal is to let demand drive the replenishment.

The buyers' role changes even more dramatically as they're no longer focused on crunching numbers and creating purchase orders. That becomes the suppliers' role. The buyers' role becomes one of policing what the supplier is recommending or sending and providing insight into the particular business while collaborating on the forecast.

There has to be a strong education program within the organisation. How does it work? What are all the commitments that have to be made by all the players on both sides of the fence? Then, how does that get you to your end goal.

Some customers report 30 to 40 per cent reductions in inventory, but the most impressive statistic of all relates to forecast accuracy: it has gone from non-existent to 75 per cent.

(*Source*: www.infochain.org)

The relationship-driven supply chain

At the end of this book, it is useful to reflect and revise on the key aspects that we believe must be found in any world-class supply chain. These are as follows:

- SCM is linked to and is part of the corporate strategy.
- SCM gives added value and competitive advantage to the business.
- Cross-functional organisational structures are found.
- Information lubricates all the processes and the decision taking.
- Key areas and performance are measured.
- Lead times are checked, reviewed and evaluated regularly.
- Customer first and customer satisfaction underpin all decisions.
- A continuous improvement culture enables people development and fosters good relationships.
- External suppliers as viewed as being 'integral partners' with collaboration also being found internally within the organisation.
- Trade-off analysis is undertaken.

And finally, Emmett (*The Supply Chain in 90 Minutes*, 2005) has noted the following supply chain rules:

Supply chain rule number 1: Win the home games first
Many companies start into SCM, by working only with the closest suppliers and customers. They should however, first ensure, that all of their internal operations and activities are 'integrated, coordinated and controlled'.

Supply chain rule number 2: The format of inventory and where it is held is of common interest to all supply chain players and must be to be jointly investigated and examined
The format of inventory is raw material, sub-assemblies/work in progress or finished goods. This is often held at multiple places in the supply chain and is controlled (in theory) by many different players who are usually, working independently of each other. This results in too much inventory being held throughout the supply chain.

Supply chain rule number 3: The optimum and the 'ideal' cost/service balance will only ever be found by working and collaborating fully with all players in the supply chain
Full benefits of SCM will only come when there is an examination of all costs/service levels together with all the players. This will result in reduced lead times and improved total costs/ service for all parties in the network. This means going beyond the first tier of suppliers and looking also at the supplier's supplier and so on. It represents more than data and process; it includes mutual interest, open relationships and sharing.

Supply chain rule number 4: Time is cash, cash flow is critical and so are the goods and information flows; fixed reliable lead times are more important than the length of the lead time
The importance of lead time in inventory is seen in the expression, 'uncertainty is the mother of inventory'. The length of lead time is of secondary importance to the variability and uncertainness in the lead time. Again, an examination of lead time throughout the supply chain involving different players and interests is critically needed.

Supply chain rule number 5: The customer is the business; it is their demand that drives the whole supply chain; finding out what customers value and then delivering it is critical
The customer is the reason for the business; so continually working to serve the customer better is critical. The customer is the business, after all. But who is the customer? The traditional view is perhaps the one that has placed the order/pays the supplier's invoice; but by seeing the next person/process/operation in the chain as the customer, this means that there are many supplier/customer relationships in a single supply chain. If all of these single relationships were being viewed as supplier/customer relationships, then the whole would be very different.

Supply chain rule number 6: It is only the movement to the customer that adds the ultimate value; smooth continuous flow movements are preferable
The movement to the customer, undertaken as quickly as possible whilst accounting for the associated cost levels, is really all that counts in adding value.

Supply chain rule number 7: Trade-off by looking holistically at all the supply chain players
There are many possibilities and opportunities available to integrate/coordinate/control across the supply chain networks: start by 'winning the home games first' in and between the internal functions; followed by all of the external connections to the supply chain networks.

Supply chain rule number 8: Information flows lubricate the supply chain; using appropriate ICT is critical
Information is required at every stage of the supply chain and for all of the levels of supply chain planning. All parts of the supply chain rely on ICT in the planning, operational, administrative and management processes.

We have tried in this book to show how these supply chain key aspects and rules are better placed and enabled by having effective and efficient relationships in the supply chain. This can and usually will, mean, changing the way of thinking and approaching how the supply chain is to be managed.

THINKING, STRUCTURING AND MANAGING

The way of thinking and the way the supply chain is structured and managed are critical. The reported benefits of following a relationship-driven supply chain approach have already been documented earlier and it will be noted that different approaches and structures do give significantly different results:

	No supply chain: functional silos	Internal integrated supply chain	Plus, external integration to the first level only
Inventory days of supply (indexed)	100	78	62
Inventory carrying cost (% sales)	3.2 %	2.1 %	1.5 %
On-time in-full deliveries	80 %	91 %	95 %
Profit (% sales)	8 %	11 %	14 %

It will be seen that by following a more integrated supply chain approach, the inventory costs fall, and profit and service fulfilment increases – the best of both worlds for the company undertaking the approach. This is why supply chain approaches have been actively pursued by those companies looking for lower costs and improved service levels. It is very clear that SCM works.

But many companies will choose consciously to remain with the power-based 'winner takes all' supply chain approaches of the adversarial pursuit of 'value for me alone' and will remain content with integrating at the first level only. This clearly may be appropriate and be seen as good business when the measure of success remains as 'profit for me alone'.

However, in a future of market-driven forces and increased uncertainty, one wonders how long companies having old established structures and holding such one-sided views will survive without re-structuring internally and without having to find new strengths externally beyond themselves. Releasing the strengths of collaboration and cooperation externally will arguably only happen when such players will also get a benefit.

Thinking differently and looking for more creative and innovative ways to manage the supply chain may therefore be a future only a few companies are able to undertake. For example, moving to more collaborative approaches involves win/win and involves trust; this remains a most difficult aspect for those left-brained rational thinking companies who prefer to use the German word for partnership of 'partnershaft'. As Alan Waller states:

> The supply chain lies no longer with an individual company; we have global networks cutting across countries and organisations. The only way to achieve this is to get players working to a common agenda – the collaboration agenda. We have been taught to compete: nobody has taught us to work together. The need and awareness is there but still nobody is taught how to do it.

It would seem a possibility that supply chain development may well falter because of the prevalent way of management thinking. There is a Welsh saying: 'Adversity comes with learning in its hand.' It could be painful to wait for the adversity and the associated hard lessons of learning from mistakes. One thing is very sure: what worked for many years may not work for many more. Therefore there is a real challenge to learn anew and, in so doing, to change. Learning and changing are indelibly connected; you cannot have one without the other.

Model for developing supply chain relationships

To take forward some of the concepts and ideas presented in this book, it can be useful to have a model to follow. The following model attempts to do this.

This model is comprehensive, accordingly, only some aspects will apply to specific situations. The use of such a model is helpful to recognise that all aspects are covered and that the right questions are asked.

Using the model with the appropriate sections in this book, will enable a complete practical application and if you follow the points through, you should have a comprehensive approach mapped out that will enable you to develop supply chain relationships in an effective way. Remember that there is a continuous nature to many of the steps, and that some will be repeated.

WHY CONSIDER IT?

- Are bought in products/services more than 50 per cent of our turnover?
- Can supplies be a source of competitive advantage?
- What are the real drivers for considering making the change?
- In three years, will existing suppliers be able to meet all our requirements?
- Do we need to develop new suppliers?
- Do we need suppliers that are more responsive?
- Are we prepared to be more responsive to our suppliers?
- Are we prepared to treat suppliers as partners?

HOW IS THE SUPPLY CHAIN MANAGED?

- Is it linked to and part of the corporate strategy?
- Is it seen as giving added value and competitive advantage to the business?
- Are there cross-functional organisational structures?
- Will we ensure that information lubricates all the processes and the decision taking?
- Are key areas and performance measured?
- Are lead times checked, reviewed and evaluated regularly?
- Does 'customer first' and 'customer satisfaction' underpin all decisions?
- Do we adopt a continuous improvement culture that enables people development and fosters good relationships?
- Are external suppliers viewed as being 'integral partners' with collaboration also being found internally in the company?
- Is trade-off analysis undertaken?

WHAT ARE THE BENEFITS AND DRAWBACKS?

- Look at the benefits and drawbacks.
- List five benefits you can see.
- List five drawbacks you can see.
- Debate/discuss/evaluate these.
- Determine whether to proceed or to drop it.
- However, if deciding to drop it, before doing this, please review the following steps.

WHAT APPROACH WILL BE USED?

- As the changes are likely to be fundamental, what overall type of approach will be needed:
  - high level of urgency, but with low resistance – this will need a more visionary/ charismatic approach;
  - crisis/low resistance – this needs a more visionary/persuasive approach;
  - high urgency/high resistance – this needs a more visionary/coercive approach;
  - crisis/high resistance – this needs an autocratic, almost dictatorial approach.
- Do those you wish to involve, have the ability to participate?
  - Are they motivated to participate?
- Does involvement (or lack of it) fit the cultures of the organisations involved?
- How important is the post-change motivation of your and your suppliers' employees?

WHAT ARE THE REASONS FOR RESISTANCE?

- What threats are those affected likely to feel?
- Will there be resentment of the imposed change?
- Do you understand the emotional aspects of those resisting the change?
- Do you understand the steps involved in people's behaviour during change?
- Have you considered reducing resistance by using:
  - participation
  - communication
  - training?

WHAT ARE THE IMPACTS OF MAKING THE CHANGE?

- Have you assessed the implications and effects of the change?
- Have you used 'force field analysis' or other approaches to think through all aspects of the change?
- For the following, have you considered all aspects of the change to the organisation's:
  - tasks
  - people
  - structure
  - culture
  - goodwill
  - information systems
  - procurement/buying process
  - manufacturing/production process
  - distribution process
  - marketing process
  - KPIs and control systems
  - reward systems.
- Have you thought through, which of the above elements have to change, and how these may in turn affect the other elements?

WHAT ARE THE INTERNAL ISSUES?

- Will you form a multi-disciplinary project team, for example: one senior manager with purchase, production, distribution and marketing representation as well as having the appropriate and similar representation from supplier(s)?
- Explore the following:
  - Consider one supply chain, or all of the supply chains?
  - Is the remit agreed and clear?
  - Who is to be involved/consulted?
  - What are the core values of the philosophy?
  - Does this fit with the current company cultures?
  - How will we evaluate suppliers?
  - What resources are needed for this programme?
  - Is a multi-functional approach valid?
  - How will effective communications be developed?
  - How will trust be developed?

- — What training is needed for our and our suppliers' employees?
- — Do we need a best supplier award?
- — How will we be consistent in practising the philosophy?
- Develop a vision/mission statement, ensuring it is:
  - — credible;
  - — challenging;
  - — consistent in all parts;
  - — clear;
  - — an integral part of the company culture;
  - — providing a bridge from the past to the future;
  - — something that all project team members believe in whole-heartedly.
- Quantify objectives.
- Develop an action plan.
- Detail resources and responsibilities.
- Define implementation mechanisms.
- Develop a 'statement of principles'.
- Agree the start date.
- Agree the project team future.

GET THE MESSAGE ACROSS

- Have you determined how to get going?
- How can you demonstrate your own belief in the vision?
- How will you use personal contact to communicate the vision?
- Will you use workshops and conferences?
- How can opportunities for two-way communication be created?
- What communication media will be used to support the messages?
- How can you use everyday meetings to build the vision?
- Have you considered using external public relations?
- How will you seek out and use examples of success?
- Have you thought through the detailed implementation actions to make the change happen, including:
  - — strategies to implement the vision
  - — short-term plans and budgets to turn strategies into action plans?

HELP PEOPLE THROUGH

- How will support be given to those working with you to implement the change?
- Will coaching be provided when it is needed?
- How are key people empowered?
- How will praise and thanks be given when appropriate?
- How will people be helped and assisted after making mistakes and failing (which is a natural part of change and of learning)?

MONITOR AND CONTROL THE CHANGE PROCESS

- How will you monitor and control the change process?

KEY ISSUES ABOUT STARTING OUT

- Recognise you are on a journey to a destination and a process of courtship > engagement > commitment.
- Ensure internally there is:
  - understanding
  - commitment.
- Recognise that the core concepts are:
  - suppliers are seen as assets and partners;
  - internal company processes in partnership;
  - long-term and HOT (honest-open-truthful) relationships;
  - joint views/analysis of TCO (Total Cost of Ownership), TAC (Total Acquisition Cost) and WLC/LCC (Whole Life/Life Cycle Costing).
- Anticipate problems; for example you will need:
  - more time in the early days;
  - management resources;
  - the will, and all must try, to succeed;
  - to exchange information;
  - to use open communication;
  - to listen before acting;
  - to receive criticism;
  - to understand people's behaviour.
- Recognise that major barriers are:
  - trust (historical mistrust will remain until the 'new' trust is formed);
  - sharing information (information will be seen as power);
  - 'The most powerful player is seen as wielding the big stick'.
- Maybe it is better to start out by selecting a supplier/product group that will give an early and visible win/win?

AND FINALLY

- Have you thought how you will motivate by giving recognition to those playing a part in the change process?
- Are you emotionally prepared to deal with all the unexpected things that will crop up, and all the matters you should have thought of but overlooked?
- And finally, have you:
  - a clear understanding of the change?
  - evidence to support the need for the change?
  - assessed the levels of support you are likely to receive from your boss and the top management of the organisation?
  - considered the value of finding a champion for the change from the ranks of top management?
  - examined ways that you can get key managers on your side through using participation approaches?
  - understood the dangers that face a specialist unit that is implementing change, but is otherwise isolated from the organisation?
- It is rarely easy changing 'the way we have always done things around here', so do not:
  - embark on a programme lightly;

- — abandon it easily;
- — begin unless senior management know what could happen;
- — begin unless senior management support it fully and openly.
- Ensure that you do:
  - — match actions and words;
  - — publicise success;
  - — anticipate problems;
  - — expect eventual success.

Bibliography

ACAS: *Effective Organisation: The people factor.* 2003.

Anderson H and Lilliecreutz J: 'The Change in Supply Chain Innovation', 19th Annual IMP Conference, Lugano. 2003

Balle M: *The Business Process Re-engineering Toolkit.* 1997

Balle M: *Systems Thinking.* 1994

Bell S: Letter in *Management Today.* March 2004

Best Factory Awards. 2001 (www.bestfactoryawards.co.uk)

Borg Instruments: 'Use of bid handicaps to stimulate supplier performance'. Borg Instruments case study (www.cips.org)

British Gas case study: CIPS Technical Publication (www.cips.org)

Brown A: 'Corporate social responsibility', *Supply Management.* 2005

Carlzon J: *Moments of Truth.* 1987

Carter R J: 'Seven Cs of effective supplier evaluation', *Purchasing and Supply Management.* April 1995

Christopher M: *Logistics and Supply Chain Management,* 2nd edition. 1998.

Covey S: *The Seven Habits of Highly Effective People.* 1990

Cox et al.: 'Power games', *Logistics Europe.* June 2003

Department of Trade and Industry: *Partnerships with People.* 1997

Director magazine. January 1994

Drucker, P: *The Daily Drucker.* 2004. (This is a compendium and therefore includes extracts from most of Peter Ducker's books.)

Ellram L: *International Journal of Project Management,* Vol. 31/2, pp. 10–16. 1995

Emmett S: 'Getting the people right', *CILT Focus.* April 2003

Emmett S: *Excellence in Warehouse Management.* 2005

Emmett S: *The Supply Chain in 90 Minutes.* 2005

Emmett S: *Improving Learning for Individuals and Companies.* 2002

Fisher R, Brown S: *Getting Together.* 1998

Goldratt E: *The Goal.* 1986 (Most of Goldratt's books are very useful.)

Jones O: *Political Procurement in Supply Management.* 1999

Meadows, D H: *Limits to Growth.* 1972

Michaels L: Letter in *Management Today.* March 2004

McGuffog T: *Globalisation in Supply Management.* 2001

McKinsey: *Quarterly Survey of Global Business Executives.* June 2005

PRTM Management Consultants: 'Managing supply chains in the 21st century' (article on website: www.prtm.com)

Parsons W: 'Heart of the matter', *Supply Management.* 15 June 2000

Porter M: *Gaining Competitive Advantage.* 1985

Saunders A: 'Supplier audits as part of a supplier relationship', *TQM Magazine,* Volume 6. 1994

The Performance Measurement Group: *Signals of Performance,* Volume 4, Number 2, 2003

'UK manufacturing supply chains', *Storage Handling and Distribution.* December 2002

'RFID', *Storage Handling and Distribution.* May 2004

Speckman D E: 'US Buyers Relationship with Pacific Rim Suppliers', *CAPS Focus Study.* 1989

Stuart F and McCutcheon D: 'Sustaining strategic supplier alliances', *International Journal of Operations and Production Management,* Vol. 16/10. 1995

Waller A: Face-to-face feature, *Logistics Europe.* March 2005

Walton S: *The Wal-Mart Philosophy.* 1992

Whitehead M: 'Corporate social responsibility', *Supply Management.* 2002

Wolstenholme A: 'Terminal velocity', *Human Resources.* November 2004 (www.hrmagazine. com)

Index

About the Authors

Barry Crocker has a background in UK freight transport and logistics. He entered full time academia in 1988 and is currently the MSc programme leader for Purchasing, Logistics and Supply Chain Management courses at the University of Salford. In addition to this, Barry undertakes training assignments worldwide and has worked with Stuart on many of these. It was during such work that the ideas for the book were formed. Barry has also written and contributed to many distance learning manuals, has been a CIPS Examiner, and is an external examiner for other universities.

Stuart Emmett has a background in freight, warehousing, shipping, and international trade and has resided in both the UK and in Nigeria. Since 1998 he has been an independent mentor/ coach, trainer and consultant trading under the name of Learn and Change Limited. Stuart currently enjoys working all over the UK and on four other continents, principally in Africa and the Middle East, but also in the Far East and South America. Additional to undertaking training, he is also involved with one to one coaching/mentoring, consulting, writing, assessing along with examining for professional institutes' qualifications and as an external MSc examiner for Purchasing and Logistics. He can be contacted at www.learnandchange.com.

Join Our E-mail Newsletter

Gower is widely recognized as one of the world's leading publishers on management and business practice. Its programmes range from 1000-page handbooks through practical manuals to popular paperbacks. These cover all the main functions of management: human resource development, sales and marketing, project management, finance, etc. Gower also produces training videos and activities manuals on a wide range of management skills.

As our list is constantly developing you may find it difficult to keep abreast of new titles. With this in mind we offer a free e-mail news service, approximately once every two months, which provides a brief overview of the most recent titles and links into our catalogue, should you wish to read more or see sample pages.

To sign up to this service, send your request via e-mail to info@gowerpub.com. Please put your e-mail address in the body of the e-mail as confirmation of your agreement to receive information in this way.

GOWER